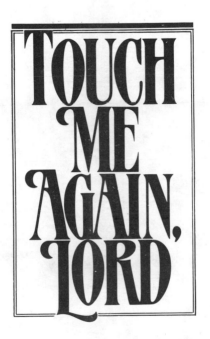

TOUCH ME AGAIN, LORD

TOUCH ME AGAIN, LORD

Ruthe White

HERE'S LIFE PUBLISHERS, INC.
P.O. Box 1576 • San Bernardino, CA 92402

TOUCH ME AGAIN, LORD
by Ruthe White

Published by
HERE'S LIFE PUBLISHERS, INC.
P.O. Box 1576
San Bernardino, CA 92402

Library of Congress Catalog Card 82-084453
ISBN 0-89840-038-4
HLP Product No. 95-044-4
© Copyright 1983, Here's Life Publishers, Inc.
All rights reserved.
Printed in the United States of America.

Note: The names of persons and locations used in this book
have been changed to protect the privacy of the individuals,
except where permission was given by those involved.

Except where otherwise indicated, all Scripture quotations are
from the New American Standard Bible, © The Lockman Foundation 1960, 1962, 1963, 1968, 1971, 1972, 1973, 1975, and
are used by permission.

Lovingly dedicated

to my husband, Claude, from whom I plagiarized much

of this material. Without his input into this manuscript

it could never have been completed.

CONTENTS

PART I   TOUCH ME

PART II   CHANGE ME

PART III   SEND ME

ACKNOWLEDGMENTS

To Bill Noller and Doug Weaver for
believing in me;

to Jean Bryant for investing so much
of her time and energy into the editing
of this manuscript;

to Les Stobbe for helping to make this
book possible.

PART ONE

Touch Me

Then *again* He laid His hands upon his eyes; and he looked intently and was restored, and *began* to *see* everything clearly (italics added).

—Mark 8:25

1

The Second Touch

Cathy's dark brown almost-curly hair lay shoulder-length against her coffin pillow. *She was such a pretty girl!* I thought as I sat listening to her funeral service. Many times since that day I have thought of Cathy, and I have always suspected that she died from the want of love!

I had gone to the hospital to be with her the morning before her death. Hours of silence rolled by as I prayed that a member of her family would walk into the room.

No one came!

At one point she turned to me, reached out her hand and said, "If only my mother would come." Within a few hours, Cathy died.

Perhaps her beauty had something to do with the tragedy of her untimely death, for the events leading to that day are mysteriously sad. Yet we shall never really know why she died, because no one ever investigated the cause.

No one seemed to need love more than Cathy did, and few have struggled to reach for it more than she. Like all of us, she longed to be loved, nurtured, and *touched*. In fact, a telephone conglomerate — recognizing that need — has built a commercial around the theme: "Reach out and *touch* someone."

Extensive psychological research verifies the human need for touching. Rene' Spitz, a psychiatrist-physician, did a study (1946) to determine the effects upon infants whose mothers withheld affection or were unable by reason of absence to provide their children with a loving environment. Her studies revealed a remarkable difference between children whose mothers fondled and touched them during the first two years of their lives and those whose mothers did not. It also showed that the mortality rate among children living in foundling homes was much higher than among children who were being raised by their own mothers.

Spitz says, "The high mortality rate is but the extreme consequence of a general decline, both psychological and physical, which is shown by children completely starved of emotional interchange." She applied the term *marasmus* (a wasting away of the body, associated with inadequate or inadequately assimilated food) to describe her findings as related to the emotionally deprived child.[1]

This psychological study verifies our need to be touched and to touch others. But let us not forget the need we also have for God's touch! We need Him to meet us and touch us where we hurt, for it is in that loving-touching relationship between Him and us that we grow. That growth becomes reality when our eyes are opened not only to our own needs, but also to the needs of others.

If we are to be effective in touching others, we need God's touch. Sometimes it is essential that He touch us, not just once, but again and again. We then become more and more able to see people with a clearer perspective, and their needs become our own.

Mark, one of the apostles, gives us the account of a man whose life was changed—but he needed a *second touch* (Mark 8:25-50). Not only was his vision clouded in relation to himself and others, he was also blind to the challenge of what was to become his new "beginning." As a result of *two* touches from the Lord, he was able to see the world around him, leave his past, and let God change him.

The event took place in a city called Bethsaida, situated beside the Sea of Galilee. The name meant "fishing house," and was derived from those whose livelihood depended upon catching and marketing fish within the surrounding region. Three of the Lord's disciples—Philip, Andrew and Peter—were fishermen by trade and had lived there. It was from those shores they had left their nets and boats to follow Jesus.

The trio of apostles were not the only persons of renown from this semi-desert city.

Mark tells of a blind man who also dwelt there. One would assume from the biblical account that Bethsaida was the blind man's birthplace. We do know he came into the city to beg alms, which was his only source of income. Historically, we are told the man wore a beggar's cloak. which was his "business license." The cloak gave him the privilege of begging alms within the city limits.

Perhaps if the blind man could tell us his story, it would be something like this:

"I often slept just outside the walls of the city and entered its gates in the morning. There I would sit, day after day, always in the same spot. Weeks rolled into years and I was no longer a stranger to those who came by. We had long since learned to tolerate each other. They had grown weary of my begging, and I of their loud voices as they haggled over their wares. Being on the streets was not a pleasant experience for me! Always, the smell of too-long-dead fish mingled with the stale body odor of weary travelers who passed by me.

"I came into the city early one morning and braced myself against the half-shaded wall of the gate entrance. There I sat to await the hustling mob of traders and worshipers. Soon I could hear the clippety-clop of a donkey's feet, and the steps of the person leading him down the street. In the background the ox-drawn carts rattled along the dirt path which led into the city. The cart's wheels screeched each time they stopped and started again. All the noises around me made me wonder: *Could this be a good omen for me?*

"When I heard people coming near me, I lifted my tin cup into the air, as I had done many times before, and cried out, 'a farth-i-n-g for the blind!' But by midday the cup was still empty and I felt defeated! The hot sun was beating down on my head and I was weary. I sat there alone, hoping some trader would have pity upon me.

"Suddenly, a hand took hold of mine and I felt myself being pulled up from the place where I was sitting. Three men whispered to each other softly as they led me out through the gate.

"'Where are you taking me?' I asked.

"'We are taking you to Jesus,' the man said. I had heard about Him and knew some had called Him an imposter. The three men escorted me outside the town. I learned later Jesus would perform no miracles inside the city's walls. He had cursed Bethsaida because the people had failed to believe in Him (Matthew 11:21).

"After the men walked with me a short distance they stopped, and the hand of another man *touched mine.* I knew it was none of the three men, for the touch was unlike anything I had felt before. Then someone placed a hand on my eyes and I began to see! Blurred images that seemed like trees were moving before my eyes. *He reached out and touched me again* — and I began to see everything clearly!"

What Did The Blind Man Begin To See?

The man, once blind, was seeing people clearly. This tells us more about his own condition than that of the persons he was viewing. He not only began to see them as people, but as something more than inanimate objects designed to meet *his* needs.

How often we, like him, grope through life with a distorted image of others. What a tragedy when we see our spouses or parents or friends as little more than "need-meeters." When that is our view, we look at them as if they were created only to accommodate us, to fill the meaningless void in our lives and to fulfill our whims. Those expectations are both unrealistic and unfair! Yet, when those around us are unable to fill our cup of beggary, we often are tempted to walk out on the relationship. It is then that both we and they may need His *second touch*. The moment God touches us, He lays an imperative upon us, an imperative of action that challenges us to become a part of life and His Kingdom on earth! Spiritual growth and development come to us as we begin to see not only our needs, but where we are in relation to the world and others around us. In order for us to be able to do this, we will need to get up from our "blind man's pallet," or whatever may be holding us, and involve ourselves with others. It may mean leaving something behind.

What The Blind Man Would Leave

Once the man received his sight, he was able

to see the dirty garments that had clothed him. They were to become the symbol of his past identity – one to which he could no longer cling. When he looked at those clothes, he faced the greatest of all challenges: Could he leave the old attachments behind? There was his cup, the cup of beggary, which he would no longer need. Could he walk away and leave it, or would he go back to the city in search of it? It was, after all, the only life he had ever known.

The decision was his!

While we cannot be sure of his reaction to the challenge, we can be reasonably sure a great deal of courage was involved. We also know it must have taken a lot of personal will power for the beggar to orient himself to the mainstream of activity unfamiliar to him. That in itself would lay new demands upon him. He, who had once been fed, would now be able to experience the joy of feeding others. What a turn-around, and what a time of new beginnings!

Whenever God *touches* us, there is that challenge to start over, to make another effort to step into the place of renewed privileges. Such effort involves us in the act of living and brings the real problem of our lives – ourselves – into clear focus! It is then we begin to recognize that we must become responsible for our own choices and actions.

After having read my book, *Be the Woman You Want to Be,* a woman wrote me to share how God dealt with her in the area of personal responsibility for her actions:

> Several months ago I sustained a back injury. It appeared, at the time, that the damage to my spine would be permanent. I was able to cope with the problem at first. Later I became resentful because I did not understand the months of extreme pain.
>
> In fact, the longer my illness dragged on, the more resentment I felt. It resulted in bitterness toward God, healthy people and myself.
>
> While reading chapter seven of your book, I sensed God touching me. I began to realize I was using my illness as a crutch, causing me to be lazy and apathetic toward life.
>
> I knew I had to take personal responsibility for making some changes. Thank you for pointing me in the right direction. I know the Lord will help me to a place of spiritual recovery in Him.

Like that woman, we also are challenged to accept the miracle of His touch in the "hurting" areas of our lives. Just as she and the blind beggar had to make a choice to leave their past behind, so must we. That choice is seldom easy, but we know we cannot follow Him without leaving something behind. Often, it is something we once held dear to us! To leave it requires a great deal of honesty and an openness of mind as we willingly follow Christ.

When the blind man made his decision to accept healing, a new life opened up to him. The restoration of sight helped him to see himself, but he could not enjoy his sightedness nor become a successful person until he was able to leave the tokens of his old beggary on the dusty streets of the past. Paul, the apostle, knew the secret of successful living. He shares it with us when he says we must press on, "forgetting what lies behind and reaching forward to what lies ahead" (Philippians 3:13). Only then can we go on.

The Blind Man Saw Jesus and He Went Home

What were the emotions of the man who once was blind? How did he feel when he saw Jesus? His feelings – and his view of Jesus – must have been unique. I doubt that the disciples were able to see Jesus on the same level as did the man who was healed. What he felt could never be understood by people who had never stumbled through crowded streets in search of a place to beg, who had never endured the indignity of wearing a beggar's cloak, who had never groped through years of blindness. Only the beggar could reckon with the individuality and the personal demands of God's touch.

One demand was an imperative: "Go home! Do not even enter the village" (Mark 8:26). Why would Jesus tell him to return home? One reason was that He did not want the man to get caught up in the miracle of the *touch*. Now that he was healed, the purpose of his life must be to obey the Lord's command without questioning – just go!

That principle is also true for us. As God touches us, He seeks to change our lives and to send us to touch others. But before we can accept His challenge to go to others, we must first be willing to let Him *touch the untouchables* — the places of our deepest hurt — regardless of what they are.

CONTACT POINT

READ: Matthew 11:21; John 9; Mark 8

1. List the areas of your greatest needs.

disciplined in eating/exercise, time; focusing on God at all time

2. Give three reasons you feel you need help in these areas.

a. *I continue to gain weight & I hate it.*

b. *I feel I waste much time — could be used more effectively*

c. *When I don't feel good, I tend to blow God off.*

3. Ask yourself: Am I willing to take personal responsibility for any negative feelings I might have concerning the "hurts" of my life? *yes*

a. Do I want to be healed?

yes

b. Am I willing to let God touch me in those
   areas? *yes*

c. Will I let go of them?
   yes - daily

4. What do you think was the blind man's
   greatest need? *trust Jesus - no*
   Tell why you think so. *This way he
   couldn't use his blindness as a
   crutch. Had to step out because of what
   *
5. Describe what God has communicated to *you*
   you while reading the above Scriptures, and *did.*
   in this chapter of the book. *When I ask
   Christ to deal w/ certain parts of me, I
   better be willing to jump out in faith.*

APPLIED LEARNING

1. How does this apply to me? *When I ask the
   Lord to change various areas of my life, I
   better be willing to do my part.*
2. What is my part in accepting healing?
   *Continuing to trust Him, no matter
   how I feel.*
3. Am I willing to take the risk for growth by
   sharing what I have learned with someone
   who may not know Christ as his or her personal Savior? (If not, ask God to help you
   by praying this simple prayer:)

   "Lord, I thank you for coming to me at the
   point of my need, for the forgiveness of my sin
   and your healing *touch*. Now, help me to go in
   your strength as I reach out to *touch* others."

[1]John C. Wright, ed., *Child Psychology*, Englewood Cliffs, NJ: Prentice-Hall, Inc., 1971, p. 105.

2

Touch the Untouchables of My Life

There was, for many years, an *untouchable* in my life. It was something I wanted to give to God, but I couldn't. After struggling with the difficulty for a long while, I became unwilling to think about it or talk about it — even to God!

I don't really know why this situation became an untouchable. Perhaps my youthfulness prevented me from fully understanding the circumstances; I was only four years old when my baby sister, Mary, was born with Down's Syndrome. I did not have adequate information about Mary's disorder, and it left me with an unspoken mystery: *Why did God do this?* I wondered.

Later, when I discovered that Mary's mental age would not exceed the level of a three-year-old child, other questions loomed before me: *Will I, being closest to her in age, always be linked with her retardation? Can I hope for a personal identity of my own?*

I can remember many beautiful moments Mary and I spent together. She had the kind, loving personality so typical of those with Down's, and she was easy to love. But the deep love I felt for her only added to the misery of this untouchable in my life. I seemed to be caught in the middle of something too big to understand, for there were painful recollections that seemed to go hand-in-hand with the lovely memories. I wanted to forget the times her dress was pinned to mine so she couldn't run away — but I couldn't forget. I couldn't run away, either, and I felt trapped between a sister I loved and my own search for personal acceptance.

My feelings of inferiority and loneliness and my desire for self-identity were compounded when my mother became a semi-invalid. She was unable to assume the home duties and to care for Mary, so I was taken out of school at age 12 to help care for them. Mother's illness and Mary's developmental disability became the focal point of my life. Caring for them was a responsibility I could not escape. The always-present situation left me with feelings of deprivation.

I yearned for an education. I felt dumb; I thought that no matter how much I read, it would never be enough. The need to know more created an insatiable hunger for learning that ate at the very marrow of my bones. It was like a fire that could not be extinguished. Often at night I would dream of going to school, only to awaken the next morning and find myself still on the farm — locked into my psychological bondage.

During my early teen years Daddy decided to move the family to California. I thought we were moving to the land of paradise because I had heard that in California a state law required all children under 16 to be in school. Being two years under the requirement, I fully expected the authorities to demand that I attend. But because we were migrant farm workers, my hopes for an education were dismal.

Two summers later it seemed that my dreams of an education were about to be realized. Mary had adapted to her surroundings quite well, and Mom seemed stronger. I enrolled as a high school freshman, but after the first semester my mother suffered a relapse. Because Mary required so much personal attention, I had to drop out of school again. My married sisters were living nearby and they helped when they could, but the responsibility of keeping Mary near me and the emotional agony of watching my mother suffer were overwhelming. Once more my dreams had to wait, and to protect my fragile identity, I built another wall of self-consciousness.

Years later, long after I was married, the opportunity came for me to re-enter school. Though the quality of my education was limited, it did provide me with a sense of self-worth. When I walked across the platform on the night of my graduation, I felt as if a burden was gone from me forever. A wave of relief swept over me.

I was soon to discover that even that satisfaction was short-lived! No matter how much I hoped the past was gone — and that I would no longer have to explain why I was a school drop-out — the hurt did not go away. My past was ever with me, hiding like a skeleton in the closet of my memory, waiting to be discovered. I knew that sometime, somewhere, someone would remember me as Ruthe, the girl with what some had called the "crazy sister."

Long after Mary died at 22, I continued to find myself emotionally tied to her, just as I had been when our clothes were pinned together. Inevitably upon making a new acquaintance my first reaction was to think, *if they really knew me, would they accept me?* It was a feeling that persisted for many years.

Now, as I speak to women of all backgrounds at seminars and retreats, I am discovering that my feelings are not uncommon. People tell me that they, too, have undergone similar emotional traumas. You may be where I was, wrestling with an untouchable hidden within the confines of your inner self. Your untouchable is probably different from mine, but it is just as real.

It could be you are unable to forgive yourself for a sin you committed at some time in your past. Maybe someone mistreated you and you feel bitterness or hatred toward that person. Perhaps an incident over which you had no control victimized you, yet you somehow feel responsible as it haunts your memory!

You may have buried those hurts deeply —

just as I did — because to be reminded of them brings intense anguish. As a result, you will not *touch* your pain; you will not permit anyone else to *touch* it, and you doubt that God can do anything about it. In spite of all your efforts to deny and to escape your pain, life itself has become a constant reminder of the hidden — almost violent — torture of unresolved guilt or sorrow that hangs over your head.

Unfortunately, painful memories don't just go away, nor does the guilt of past errors. Unless we let God deal with those things, they become mounting sources of frustration. They never leave us! They are always in our subconscious minds.

Sometimes other people unwittingly bring our pain to the conscious level, and we — who thought those things were closed off — swallow our pride and turn away to bleed alone. We look for comfort in the private silence of our thoughts. It is a retreat we know too well, a solitude enjoyed until it is broken by the dreadful thunderings of our spirit demanding to be free.

In the past I often chose that aloneness with myself, retreating to my secret psychological hiding place. There in the cocoon of my inferiority I felt safe. But I wasn't!

Sometimes when I spoke at luncheons or retreats or seminars, women would come to me, not understanding my background, and say, "It's all right for you to talk about motivation and rising above the hurts of life, but what do you know about *real* hurting?"

Such questions forced me to deal with myself. I would stand there, my heart shriveling up inside me, wanting to share, to tell them. But I was afraid to do so. Part of me wanted release; the rest of me was fearful. I was unable to face the responsibility of dealing with my pain objectively. I knew I needed God's help to resolve my problem.

Yet I also knew that even with His enablement, it would not be easy for me to break loose from the chains of my past. The walls I had built to insulate myself would have to come down; and the barriers of inferiority, behind which I had hidden, must be removed. But when I tried, there always seemed to be another block, or another fence to hurdle. Somewhere there had to be a release. I longed for it—but I was unable to find it. *Can I rise above these feelings of inferiority,* I wondered, *and even above my possible lack of social unacceptability?*

Lord, I Want to Be Healed

I really wanted healing, but before it could come, I would have to be willing to come before God in open honesty. I would have to allow His help to reach the depth of my need. His touch, however real, would not produce its effect until I permitted His healing to take place inside me. When I did, something happened. God performed a work in me!

One day I was speaking to a group of ladies, and I knew it was time to share my background with them. I shared my need to let go of the past, and made myself vulnerable to them. God touched me in that moment, and in the days that followed, I began to see that a process of healing had begun.

First, I had to learn to accept the unchangeables in my life so that I could be motivated to become more than I was. I came to realize that my entire life was centered around something about which I could do nothing. I could not change the disability of my baby sister. I could not change the choices of my parents. I could not change the fact that I had to earn my high school diploma in a way that did not measure up to my dreams.

If God were going to help me transform the negative past into a positive framework for the present, I knew I had to be willing to let go of it. My heart was willing, but the fleshly nature of my ego was weak. Yet, as I took each faltering step, God helped me.

The development was a gradual one as God dealt with me in a painstakingly slow, but loving, way. I know now the reason He chose to work with me in that manner; I was much too fragile to have survived the emotional shock of a cataclysmic release.

A counselor friend of mine explained it to me like this: We are like an onion with its many layers. The outer tissue is only the tough covering which protects what is on the inside. God's first touch breaks that hardened layer loose. He then keeps "peeling" away at our built-up hurts.

Before He begins that work in us He always asks, "Will you be made whole?" That is the very question He placed before the man at the Pool of Bethesda (John 5:2-15). Why would the Lord inquire of him in such a manner? The man had been brought there for many years. He had come for the express purpose of finding healing.

The answer to our Lord's query is found in the man's reply. "Sir, I have no one to put me in the water. . ." The sick man was not unlike us. We, too, are prone to blame others for our own inadequacies. By so doing, we seek to absolve ourselves of any personal responsibility. Since the current thought of sociology gives us permission to blame someone else — society, government or the church — we look for a culprit upon whom we can place guilt. We, then, stay right where we are, immobile, waiting for someone to come along and perform a miracle in us. . .one that will bring an instant, total recovery.

Women who have assumed that spiritual posture often come to me seeking quick relief from depression. When I explain to them that God wants their cooperation, some accept the challenge and others do not. They seem conditioned to believe if someone, just anyone, would perform a magical hocus-pocus trick, everything in their lives would be fine. Not so! God demands our voluntary cooperation!

Healing Involves Trust

Along with making the decision to cooperate with God in letting go of my past, I also saw my need to trust God. It sounds so easy! But we all know our past failures and present weaknesses, and it is difficult to believe He will work through us in spite of them. We may, as a result, begin to feel like a swimmer who knows all the guidelines for safety but is caught in the under-tow. Like that person, we can thrash about gasping for air, or we can lie back and relax, trusting God's sovereign power to bear us up. We might even expect Him to perform some great miracle that will rescue us from life's rip-tide.

In most cases, I find God helps me by teaching me how to help myself. He lets me go along until I have exhausted all self-energy as I flail my way through the ocean of life. Then, when I think I am about to go under for the third time, He comes to my rescue. I know He will never permit me to drown. The Lord wants me to rediscover the oft-hidden secret of trusting Him — even in the midst of prevailing pain.

There are times when no matter what we do to help ourselves, the "hurt" lingers. I was discussing this with a friend to whom this had happened. Even though he had been a Christian for many years, he was faced with a new challenge to trust God in the midst of his prevailing hurt. He told me about his challenge.

"My heart was breaking because of an incident that centered around my business. Someone lied about me and tried to defame my character. I was concerned, but not only about my personal reputation. There were other anxieties as well. My testimony in the community and how this would affect others was of much concern to me. As a result of all the turmoil going on inside me, I closeted myself away from those who loved me most. I could not face friends for fear of being misunderstood. The hurt was too deep to talk about, and to cry hurt even more!

"I came to the place, for the first time in my Christian experience, where I was unable to pray. My heart was like an iceberg, and my emotions were coldly stiff from the agony of my soul.

"Months went by before help came. Then one night, while I was asleep, the Holy Spirit ministered to me. Somewhere in the depths of my inner being there came a 'thawing' — a spiritual awakening. The wall of pent-up emotions began to melt away, and my tears flowed like water. When I awakened the next morning, I felt refreshed and knew I could trust God regarding the matter. The Lord did help and turned the situation to work in my favor. The accusers were caught in their own trap!"

Here was a man whose cry was so personal only he knew about it. On the surface he might have thought himself defeated. Not so! Instead God *touched* the *untouchable of his life.* Not only did our heavenly Father minister to the man on a personal level, He knew my friend's needs better than he knew them himself.

The writer of Romans was well aware of what it meant to carry such a personal weight. He also knew about God's provision in the time of "hurting." The apostle Paul cried out in agony when he wrote, "Wretched man that I am! Who

will set me free from the body of this death?"
(Romans 7:24). The disciple knew that every
burden must be carried by someone, and that
for one to be delivered there must be a *deliverer.*
He looked for that *one!*

Did you notice that Paul did not say, "this
body of death"? Rather, he reversed the terms:
"the body of *this* death." In so doing, Paul drew
an analogy from a life experience. He, no doubt,
had watched a street scene in ancient Rome.
We are told by some Bible commentators that
it was customary in that day to strap the body
of a dead man to the back of a prisoner. The
prisoner would then carry the corpse through
the city streets. The event was accompanied
with a celebration as the frenzied crowd followed him and mocked him.

Though Paul carried no actual body, his
burden was nonetheless real! And he knew
none of his contemporaries were willing or able
to lift the weight. Jewish law forbade touching
the dead and required a series of ceremonial
cleansings in the event one did have contact
with a corpse (Leviticus 21). For that reason
he sought a deliverer outside the realm of
human power. We can be sure he found the
Deliverer and was freed from the cumbersome
weight that prompted his soul's cry, for he
wrote that Christ Jesus had made him free
from the law of sin and death (Romans 8:2).

Spiritual freedom comes when the soul is set
free! Though the burden of pain we carried may
have been personal to us, we are no longer its
captive. God *touches* us to set us free — and He

stands ready to *touch* not just the hurting areas of our lives but much *more!*

CONTACT POINT

READ: Romans 8:26; Hebrews 4:15; Galatians 6:9; Job 17:9; 1 Corinthians 15:17

1. Are you or have you ever been where the apostle Paul was in Romans 7:24? If so, what was the circumstance?

2. How important is it to you that God deals with the "untouchables" of your life? Are you willing to give Him the chance to help you? What steps are you willing to take in cooperation with God?

3. What happens to us internally and spiritually when we refuse to let God touch us where we hurt?

4. What are some of the alternatives we sometimes use in trying to solve our own problems?

5. What are the results of those choices?

APPLIED LEARNING

1. List three of the most enjoyable moments of your life. Tell why!

2. Write the names of three persons who made the greatest positive influence in your life.

3. What characteristics of their lives made the greatest impact on you? List three ways in which you can learn from their example.

4. Contact one of them and tell him what he has meant to you in the past. Then, ask him to join you in prayer concerning the area of your life where you are struggling.

5. Confess your need to God and leave the burden with Him.

3

Lord, Touch All of Me

God is more to me than a mental or spiritual
fire escape!

He is not someone to whom I run only when
my soul is in the heat of anguish. While I know
He stands ready to help me during my life-
threatening moments, those are not the times
His touch is most essential.

I need God's touch every day of my life. The
touch may come to me in various ways—by His
Spirit, through others, and most assuredly by
His written Word. By recognizing Him on a
day-to-day basis and accepting His daily
strength, I am given confidence to trust Him
during the crisis moments. It is the on-going
relationship which often makes the difference
between my ability to trust Him—or my
tendency to panic!

Trust is the kind of understanding which
enables one person to believe in and depend

upon the other. However, because human inter-dependence often breaks down and people fail us, we have a tendency to think of God as having the same fallible nature. At times we may find it easier to trust people than put our confidence in God.

There is a visible but false security that may surround us in the interaction of family and friends. We are tempted to lean upon them, to let them become our source of help, without recognizing their human limitations. Often they, too, are struggling with much the same problems as we. The easy visibility of their presence may be comforting, but it is not adequate for meeting our needs.

On the other hand, faith in God demands we *trust* Him even when He cannot be seen. We are asked to believe there is hope when none is on the horizon, and to turn loose of our problems when the intellect is telling us to hang on to them. Human reasoning, at that moment, becomes our greatest obstacle!

This tendency to clutch at something we are better off releasing reminds me of a message Pastor Gurden Henley once wrote in his church bulletin:

> I remember when I first learned to float. I was about seven years old, and it was at David's Resort on beautiful Lake Stevens in western Washington. I was in the beginners class, receiving the free Red Cross swimming lessons. One of the first lessons a beginner learns is to float.
>
> Years later as a teenager, after having gone through all the lessons, I taught that same

beginners class. I well remember how dangerous it was trying to teach those children how to stay afloat. I would try to get them into water deep enough so they could not touch bottom, to persuade them to lie back in the water. They would cling to me, scratch me and pull my hair, in their thrashing about for something to grasp onto. What a smile came over their faces when they learned to lie back and trust the water to hold them up. Of course, once that happened, they were well on their way toward learning to swim.

We have all been there, at a place where we needed God, or where God in His loving kindness held us up. Once we have learned the secret of leaning heavily upon Him, we will understand why David said, "In thee, O Lord, do I put my trust" (Psalms 31:1, KJV).

You and I will either learn to believe in God's sovereign power and guidance, or we will flutter through life in fear and trepidation. Even for Christians, the way is not always clear — we are not immune to daily problems, and life can be perplexing.

In many respects we are in the same boat as the rest of the world. Our dollars have to buy food, clothing and shelter. The automobiles we must drive are not trouble-free. Our children get sick and our houses may have leaky roofs. We can find ourselves among the ranks of the unemployed, and it may be difficult for us to live in harmony with the "yet-to-be-perfected saints" who share our homes. Even the ever-changing culture of today's society affects us, for it touches those who are inside the religious community as well as those who are not.

But when we compare ourselves to those who have not yet known the touch of God in forgiveness, there should be a predictable difference in how we respond to life situations. His touch enables us to maintain a unique lifestyle: a lifestyle that calls for consistency in our priorities.

God's Touch Orders Our Priorities

Because as Christians our life's principles will often run counter to those of the world system, we need to be consistent in our priorities as we are faced with decisions. Did not Christ himself declare, "Seek ye first the Kingdom of God, and His righteousness" (Matthew 6:33, KJV)? We are fully aware that that concept is not in harmony with much of the conditioning of this decade. In fact, it is diametrically opposed to the selfish attitude so popular today. We may find the philosophy, "get all the gusto you can out of life" quite tolerable among the unchurched, but when that same "gimme" theology becomes the measurement for spiritual growth, it is a different matter.

My friend Annelle once told me about how she was caught up in that idea. Feeling she should have all she wanted as a Christian, she proceeded to act out her fantasy. When a well-known evangelist announced his tour to the Holy Land, she used her so-called faith as leverage, bought her ticket and paid for it with a check without sufficient funds in the bank to cover it. While abroad she "confessed" her claim that the money, by some miracle, would be deposited in her account.

It wasn't, and the woman was devastated!

With all of today's emphasis on materialism by both the world and segments of the church, we have become vulnerable to the pressures of a self-oriented lifestyle. We demand more things, we want more things, and we get more things than any other society in the history of the world. Yet, it seems we never have enough.

Today's attitudes and values differ sharply from those of earlier generations. The most pronounced changes have developed within the past three or four decades. Our grandparents and their parents needed food, clothing and shelter, but their *wants* were minimal. They lived more simply, and luxuries were almost unheard of except among the elite. Not so in our time! While we, too, need clothes to wear, food to eat and houses in which to live, we want more. We demand designer clothes, specialized foods and custom-built homes. Our so-called needs far exceed the combination of wants and needs known to former generations.

According to the greeds-equals-needs philosophy, every ounce of life's energy should be focused on getting, on finding one's own comfort. But at what cost? Of losing any real purpose for life? We need God to *touch* us in the area of our wants and needs and to help us get our priorities in order.

In an interview with a leading film writer-producer, the question of priorities was raised. The writer placed his personal need for fulfillment above everything else, including his marriage, which was named third on his list. What his idea of fulfillment was I am not sure, but I am convinced that none of us is immune to the effects of selfish, materialistic thinking. It is for that reason we need God in every aspect of our daily lives.

We Need Him Daily

It is the daily *touch* which makes the difference in our life-style. Since, according to the psalmist, God "daily bears our burden" (Psalms 68:19), should we not seek Him on a daily basis?

In His Sermon on the Mount, Jesus gave us the model prayer. In it he taught us to ask for our daily bread (Matthew 6:11). Bread, the staff of life, is always symbolic of our day's needs, whatever they may be, and Jesus told us to ask God for them! When we do, prayer becomes the *action* of our faith(ing) process, based on our need.

Each day's needs are different from those of the day before because life is not static. It is not the same yesterday, today, and tomorrow. Things around us are constantly changing, circumstances vary, and today's situations are often the reverse of yesterday's. We cannot predict the day; but we can be sure God's strength will sustain us.

When the Lord encouraged us to seek Him daily, He also reminded us that each day has enough trouble of its own. So, we shouldn't borrow anxiety, nor presuppose upon our human ability to cope with life (Matthew 6:34). That is not easy!

It is hard because when we have learned to solve our problems intellectually, we have a tendency to become smug and to feel we can handle anything. God sometimes leaves us to our ingenuity long enough for us to get up against those things about which we can do nothing. Only then do we know how much we need Him!

Recently I attended a retreat where a young singer spoke about how God taught him the lesson of day-to-day trust. "I have always been able to do things pretty much on my own," he said. "My job and career were easily managed within the framework of my highly-motivated spirit of independence until a new and different kind of problem touched my life. I was diagnosed as having an incurable disease. Suddenly, I discovered I was facing something that required His strength, not mine! It was then I learned the secret of my 'daily bread.'"

Sooner or later we all will come to that same place in life! If we do not have His touch, we will lose confidence, be filled with anxiety, and our spirit-life will wane. But we are not permanently lost; we can remember the blind man, and ask God to *touch us again*. That touch always brings new life!

God's Touch Revitalizes

God's touch in the daily routine of activities brings a revitalization to our weary bodies. His touch pours strength into our weak faith and

puts a song in our saddened hearts because it
changes how we see the circumstance and how
we see ourselves. Mainly, it is our attitude
toward life which takes on the change. Joy, a
minister's wife, shared with a group of other
women about how this principle worked in her
life. Her husband had accepted a pastorate in
a small desert community. The move involved
a great deal of change for both her and the
family.

"I didn't want to go there, didn't like the area,
and felt the people in the parish didn't like me.
Living conditions were intolerable. I was
unhappy! My husband was miserable because
I was. There were many problems with which
I had to deal. They were unlike any I had faced
before. I did not understand where I was in the
picture of my life, nor the purpose in me, or my
family, being there.

"One morning while talking to God about
how horrible the whole thing was, I felt an inner "tug" to get up from the floor where I was
praying. ᵀ stood, pulled my jogging suit onto
my overweight body, and headed up the road
near the house. There was a pebble beside the
path and it just fit the toe of my tennis shoe.
I began kicking the rock and stepping, until
I had stepped-and-kicked my way up a deep
incline.

"On my way back down, I suddenly realized
I was angry at the wrong person. It was not
God, but just the circumstances of life that had
me in a corner. Recognizing this, I said, 'Lord,
I will serve You no matter what life holds for

me. I refuse to allow the problems around me to change my attitude toward You.' No sooner had I spoken those words than something happened inside me. I had new energy, and there was a spring in my step as I made my way home. God revitalized me that day. I knew then I could do anything, accept anything, as long as He was with me. Things around me had not changed one iota, but my attitude toward things *had* changed!"

Many of us have been where Joy was. Circumstances in our lives have caused us to lose hope. We may be exhausted from the battle, for it is often in the nitty-gritty of daily life that we lose our courage. We try to control our steps and find we cannot.

We need to let God come into the everyday situation, but often we have difficulty giving those little — and not-so-little — frustrations to Him. We have to learn to take Him as our daily sustenance. The daily *touch* brings not only a revitalization of strength and purpose, but it also provides us with stability of character.

God's Touch Brings Stability and Growth

When Christ lives in us, He brings about growth and positive change. As we mature, we seek to emulate Him because "the love of Christ controls us" (2 Corinthians 5:14). God's touch comes to establish within us those growth patterns that are in harmony with His precepts. One such pattern is self-control, which provides us with stability.

It was this pattern that Jesus wanted to en-

courage in the life of the blind beggar He healed
in Bethsaida (Mark 8). After Jesus had touched
the man a second time, He told him to go
home—but not to enter the village and, according to the King James Version of the Bible, he
was not to tell anyone in the town about his
miraculous healing.

What a test of that man's stability! When
those who had known him all his life were to
ask, "Who healed you?" the former beggar
could only reply, "I cannot tell." Surely he must
have wondered why the Lord would lay such
a demand upon him.

Had this been a modern day happening, most
of us would be tempted to put a full-page ad
in the largest newspaper in the city: **BLIND
BEGGAR HEALED!** Perhaps we would consider writing a book about our experience—or
putting it on radio or television. What a cap-
tion this event would have made for the
Bethsaida Press! But Jesus said, "No!"

We know that Christ's work was not yet
finished, and He did not want the man to get
caught up in the miracle. His purpose was for
the man to become a whole person. His touch
was to control and constrain the selfish motives
of the man He healed, just as He seeks that
same purpose for our lives. Obedience to His
command always brings stability. When we
learn to obey, His cause becomes ours, His principles for daily living become our goal and we
begin to see that we have grown.

Growth comes through His *touch* because He
touches the whole of our lives. It is not a once-

in-a-lifetime "zapping," but an on-going relationship! By understanding that we do not reach maturity with one sweeping touch, we can then accept our personal imperfections. When we do accept those weak areas, we shift the emphasis from our *experience,* to the *work* God is doing in us! We begin to see that the whole of our lives is being changed to fit into the total plan of His work!

That plan will not be effective in us until the changing has begun. However gradual the progression toward Christian maturity may be, we should always be changing and growing more like Him! It is God's *touch* that makes the difference — but how does He touch us?

He Touches Us Through His Written Word

No experience is valid unless it is based upon God's written Word. This truth was made real to me when I observed another young Christian singer in his search to find God's touch. Although he was a guest in our home, the young man was not eating. After several days my husband, Claude, became alarmed about the matter and decided to talk with the singer. The young man informed Claude that he was on a prolonged fast. The two of them talked through the night into the early morning hours. After the conversation had ended, the man slipped away quietly and made his way to the church.

Fifteen years later, while attending a Christian Bookseller's Convention in Denver, Colorado, I felt someone tap me on the shoulder.

Turning around, I recognized the singer we had entertained years before.

He reached out, pulled me into his long, spindly arms and said, "Claude will never know what his talk did for me. That evening as we talked together in your living room, he made me aware of my need to trust in God's Word. I was at a crossroad in my life, and that evening was the turning point as my spiritual eyes were opened. You folk were not aware that at that time I had vowed never to eat until God revealed himself to me. What a joy when I understood my faith rested in the written Word instead of some visible manifestation of who God is."

Like that man, many of us look for God's *touch* only if we can see it with our eyes or touch it with our hands. Thomas, often called the doubting apostle, had a similar problem. He could not believe Jesus had been resurrected. He said, "Unless I shall *see* in His hands the imprint of the nails, and put *my* finger into the place of the nails, and put *my* hand into His side, *I will not believe*" (John 20:25, italics added). It was not until eight days later, as Jesus walked through the closed doors where the disciples were meeting, that the doubter came face-to-face with the Living Word. The Lord invited Thomas to touch Him, and then Thomas realized who Jesus was!

Why was it so difficult for the disciple to believe Jesus had actually been resurrected? Had the Lord not told all of His followers He would rise again? Why was His word not enough for them to base their faith upon?

We know they heard the words from our Lord with their ears, but their hearts did not comprehend the truth of it. Like most of us, they did not have a full understanding of His Word at work in them. Thomas had wanted visible proof, and his response to the presence of Jesus was a perfectly human one. The Lord did not rebuke him for his unbelief. Instead, Jesus gave the man an opportunity for growth by affirming His presence to Thomas.

When our seeking of God's touch is based on the promise of who He is — "The Word was with God and the Word was God" (John 1:1) — we begin to understand Him as the *indwelling One.* He does an inward work as His spirit bears witness with our spirit that we are His children (Romans 8:16). The affirmation of the spirit at work in us comes through the avenues of our conscience, emotions and nature itself, but they never work independently of His Word. It is through the Scripture that we are changed into His likeness, for *"We are changed into the same image from glory to glory even as by the Spirit of the Lord"* (2 Corinthians 3:18, KJV, italics added). Step-by-step, the process of growth continues as we live in His Word, allowing God to *touch* the *whole* of us: our fears, our broken dreams. . . and our doubts.

CONTACT POINT

READ: John 20:26-28; Hebrews 12

1. What do you think is meant by the words, "Blessed are they that have not seen..."?

a. To whom does this verse of scripture refer, and why?

b. How is it applicable to you personally?

c. Do you find this verse difficult to believe? If so, why?

2. Define the difference between intellectual knowledge of God and spiritual insight and believing by faith in His Word.

3. What is the definition of the word "faith" as described in Hebrews 12?

4. Why is it sometimes difficult to believe God for our "daily bread"?

5. What part do your emotions play in your attitude toward believing God's Word? Why?

APPLIED LEARNING

1. Give some incident in your life when you were unable to solve your own problems. Think about what your reactions were and write them down.

2. Has there been a time when God met your needs in a very special way? If so when, how?

3. When did you last give God thanks for all His daily provision?

PART TWO

Change Me

CHANGE ME, LORD

Change me, Lord
When I am prone to doubt,
To question
What life is all about.

Change all of me,
As you bring
My dreams
And goals
to reality.

DOUBTING IS A PERSON'S RIGHT TO QUESTION GOD — RESOLVING THOSE DOUBTS IS GOD'S WAY OF TELLING US HE CARES

4

Turn My Doubts to Belief

The staccato-like footsteps of an inconsiderate nurse marching down the hallway had awakened me early that morning. I lay on my hospital bed, fighting the debilitating weakness of a chronic kidney infection.

Through the window I could see vapors of steam rising from the ground, as the desert sun beat down upon the freshly watered lawn. Droplets of water, condensed from humidity in the air, hugged the window pane. For three days I had lain there watching as the scene repeated itself in the morning sunlight. I felt as helpless as the water clinging to the transparent window glass!

Moments later my doctor came into the room to tell me I could go home. "Don't travel any more than 30 minutes at a time without stopping to rest," he added. "And don't get overtired. Don't forget to take your medication, and don't expect too much too soon; your condition is a chronic one. Just learn to live with it."

How does one "learn to live with it?" Die, maybe...but not live! I thought to myself.

During the months that followed I was taken back and forth between my home and the hospital many times. Each bout with the illness left me weaker than the one before. Heavy daily dosages of antibiotics caused severe muscle cramps that resulted in sleepless nights. The persistent low-grade fever I carried was like my shadow — always there. How I wished the temperature would go away!

I felt haunted by my own body. It stalked me like a ghost in the night, reminding me of the possibility of another attack. There were days I wanted to die, other days I was afraid I would. Life became a see-saw — sometimes up, mostly down. I began to feel forsaken by God and misunderstood by friends.

Being ill brings a special kind of doubt. At times I found myself doubting my own ability as I questioned the loving kindness of our heavenly Father, and the purpose of life itself. I also tended to doubt the tomorrows, to fear the unknown, and to struggle with the what-ifs.

A flood of questions swept through every fiber of my being. *Why me? What is life all about, anyway? God, where are you when I need you? Do I have sin in my life* (as some well-meaning friends had tried to make me believe)? *If so, is that the cause of my illness?*

I began to search for every known and unknown sin I might have committed that would cause the sickness. Like a perfectionist housewife looking for one speck of dust, I examined the crevices of my soul looking for things that might need to be confessed. I searched desperately for the culprit, seeking healing through the mental and spiritual catharsis of my confessions.

It didn't help. I came to realize that there would be no thunder, no flash of lightning from God to reveal some hidden sin that lurked in the deep cavity of my soul. I begged Him to tell me what more I should confess, but He was silent.

Then someone sent me a booklet with a note attached. It read, "The secret of your healing is in *praise.*" *Doesn't she think I have tried that?* I fumed. Angry, I felt that I was being punished by some unseen judge who wished to lay the sentence of death upon me.

Yet I was willing to do anything for healing, and I tried the praise formula as well. For some time I made a conscious effort to praise God in everything, for I knew that the principle of praise is right and biblically sound. I listed the many things God had done for me over the past few weeks, pausing to give Him thanks again.

But I did not improve. My condition worsened and the thermometer registered a rise in my temperature. (I discovered that no matter how sound the principle of praise is, the extreme legalism of its application may be both cruel and harsh.)

The many approaches I took toward healing did little more than lead me into deeper in-

trospection and more frustration. I tried
everything! Having accepted Christ as personal Savior at the age of eight, I could quote
Bible verses like a spiritual pro. As a teacher
active in church work, I had quick answers to
everyone's needs. Yet, those answers were not
working for me. As a Christian I was trying
to put the puzzle of life together, and some of
the pieces were missing!

Then, one Sunday afternoon when my husband and our two daughters (who had lovingly cared for me during my long illness), had
gone to church, I found myself alone and
desperate. I dropped my tired body onto the
floor and began to weep. Finally, I grew weary
from my crying. Too weak to pray, I just lay
there quietly. All sense of time was lost in the
solitude of the moment.

My thoughts took me into the biblical account of where Christ appeared to His disciples,
as they were on the Sea of Galilee. I visualized
His coming to them in the midst of the storm.
He spoke *"peace"* to them. That was what I
needed! I wanted His peace to calm the troubled waters of my soul. Suddenly I knew that
even though I didn't understand life, I did know
Him! I asked to know His peace, and He gave
it to me!

The knowledge of His presence brought with
it an inner psychological and emotional healing. The turmoil inside me was gone the very
moment I became aware of His *touch*. Instead
of conflict, I felt peace — and an unquestionable
trust. It was a trust that would allow God to

be sovereign in my life. I no longer saw Him as a judge, ready to pronounce my death sentence. I gave Him my illness and surrendered all my past and present sins to His forgiving nature. That, in turn, brought a tremendous release, and I no longer felt bound by my inadequacies.

But there was no instant physical healing. No visible change took place in my life, and it was three years before my health was restored. Yet at the particular moment of His *touch*, my physical healing became less important to me than the calm assurance of God's presence. I knew God was touching me right where I was hurting. . . and doubting!

Sometimes doubt is a psychological mechanism for survival. We learn to doubt because we are unable to trust. Doubt is so closely related to our reasoning that it can easily become a part of our ego-system. When that occurs, our intellectual reasoning takes precedence over our faith. Then we must make a rational decision to resolve the doubts – but how?

How Do We Resolve Our Doubts?

We resolve our doubts as we come to God through His Word! Rick Howard, a young theology student, talked with my family about his moments of doubting the deity of Jesus. Rick was the speaker at our church during a summer "Youth Emphasis Week." As we observed the youthful minister, Claude and I sensed an unusual depth of Christian maturity about him. One evening, we all sat together talking, and he told us the secret of his dedication.

"I entered ministerial training at one of the most prestigious universities of the nation while still in my teens," he said. "Having been raised in a pastor's home, I was provided with a loving and intellectually stimulating environment.

"I had never questioned the deity of Christ prior to my entrance in the university. While there I began to doubt the miracles of the New Testament and to question Jesus' resurrection. One night as I was caught in the confusion of my own mind, I resolved to find some answers. Either the Lord was the resurrected One, or He was an impostor. I had to know! I decided that if what I had learned in the past was not truth, then I must find out what was. The battle ensued as I studied through volumes of textbooks. Finally, I threw myself into the study of the Word, and it was there my doubts were settled. The resurrected Christ *touched me, . . . again!*

Like Rick, all of us may have a time in our lives when we will doubt and be challenged to reaffirm our faith. Once we have that affirmation, it is important that we never permit ourselves to go back and re-examine what God has already established. You will remember Thomas never doubted again once he saw Jesus. He drove in what I call a "spiritual peg," and hung his doubting on it. Never again would

Thomas be called a doubter, nor would he question who Jesus was!

We all need to drive in our spiritual pegs, because they are reminders to us of how far we have come. Those same markers can determine boundary lines and establish ownership. My father was a farmer who knew a lot about "driving down the stakes." They were sticks driven into the soil by a surveyor who had carefully measured the land. The acreage had always been there, its potential was endless, but its ownership was in question until the posts were put there to determine which land belonged to whom.

Throughout the Old Testament the patriarchs were asked to lay down stones to mark their holdings and to build memorials. That seemed to be God's way of teaching them to maintain reminders of what He had done for them in the past. Jacob built his Bethel where he returned many times. His faith was always strengthened when he came back to the place of his "spiritual pegs." Abram dug wells that were memorials not only for himself, but also for his son Isaac. He knew the wells were his: they were dug on his land, and he would always fight to keep them!

Once we know our doubts are settled and the property lines of our relationship to God are clearly defined, we are then able to declare our *spiritual rights.* Three things are necessary in staking those claims: First, we must *know* what those claims are. Then, if there are any questions, they must be settled upon the basis of God's Word. Finally, we must know who made the purchase.

Members of the early Corinthian church (the people with all the gifts) had to be reminded of this very concept. The apostle Paul wrote to them, saying, "You were bought with a price; do not become slaves of men" (1 Corinthians 7:23). When we understand who owns us, we will also know our legal rights of possession. We *can* possess all the land of our potential talent and ability, as long as it is done through Him! We cannot declare our own worth; only He who bought us has that right. Since God bought us with the death of His Son, the price of our ownership has been paid in full!

Until we learn to grasp the truth that we belong to God, we will find ourselves constantly struggling in a tug-of-war over who owns whom. There always will be a "pull" when we are caught in the strain of doubt.

To Whom Do We Turn With Our Doubts?

There is only one place to go with our doubts—right back to the One who knows us best and loves us most. When John the Baptist was being held in Herod's prison, he began to doubt himself and Jesus. He sent his own disciples to go to talk directly with Jesus (Matthew 11:3). John knew, in his heart, that Jesus would tell him the truth about His Messiahship, so John asked, "Art Thou He that should come? Or do we look for another?"

How absurd that the man who had baptized Jesus, who heard the voice of God and who had seen the dove descending upon Him, was now questioning what he had seen and heard! Where was the man's faith?

But wait, before we become critical of Jesus' forerunner, let us look at the conditions which surrounded him. Where was he? John did not ask his questions from the soft cushions of a mansion overlooking the crowded sights of a metropolitan city. There were no religious leaders standing around to applaud his bravery. Instead, he cried out from the darkened hole of a prison dungeon where the morning sunlight was lost in the musty atmosphere of his confinement. There were no luxuries; not even the necessities of life were offered him.

While there in the torture of his body and soul, cut away from those he loved, his faith went into an eclipse. He wasn't sure if he was remembering correctly. Those things that once were certain had become uncertain! The Jordan River experiences were still a part of his memory, but he must have asked: *Is my memory failing me, am I going mad? Did the incidents concerning Jesus really occur?*

John's doubting stemmed from three *unavoidables* that touched his life.

He Was in a Place of Idleness

There was an unavoidable idleness imposed upon him. Doing absolutely nothing was not a part of his personality. That rugged individual who had clothed himself in camel's hair and eaten grasshoppers with wild honey was now caged in like an animal. He was hemmed in from all sides, spiritually, mentally, and physically. His soul was begging for release!

This unwilling isolation had cut him off from his own disciples. He could not confer with them during the day or speak with them at night. He who had preached that Jesus had a fan in His hand and would sweep up the floor, was now being swept away by his own doubts. He who had declared that the Lord would take care of the social injustices of the day was left alone to question the justice of his own lot. He must have thought, *Where are you, Jesus when I need you?*

The Unavoidable Of Lost Fellowship

Because he was cut off from his followers and like members of the faith, his doubting took place in the *aloneness* of his personal prison. There was nothing, no one, to divert his thoughts. He was a captive of his mental inquiries, and was left *alone* to struggle through them.

How much like him we all are. While we may not be held behind the iron gates of a penal system, it is highly possible we are imprisoned with our thoughts. The situation around us may be driving us into compulsive thinking; a mental obsession that closes us off from the realities of life. Or it could be we are in a psychological prison of our doubts because we were trying to do something for the Kingdom of God and our motives have been sorely misunderstood. As a result, the forces of opposition keep pounding away at our better judgment. We know who we are and to whom we belong, but we cannot seem to move from our point of desperation.

When we find ourselves there, desperate and isolated from the fellowship of God and friends, we must make a conscious effort to restore fellowship. Whatever the reason for being where we are, to be cut off from other believers is always damaging to our spiritual welfare. There is strength that comes through a body of believers. That is the reason for the exhortation in Hebrews which reads: "Not forsaking the assembling of ourselves together, as the manner of some is, but exhorting one another; and so much the more, as ye see the day approaching" (Hebrews 10:5, KJV).

With the emphasis there is today on small group sharing (which I think is great), I do see a danger in moving away from the regular attendance of church worship. There is something about becoming a part of the total work of God that brings us to a place of balanced spiritual growth. We should guard ourselves against moving back and forth from one group to another without ties of responsibility to a corporate body of Christian believers. Life will force us into enough corners. We dare not make additional prisons of isolation. If we do, when the moments of doubting come we will find ourselves without support systems. The extreme loneliness of our isolation will be like that of John the Baptist. It is compounded even more when the course of life is uncertain.

The Unavoidable of the Unknown

John could do nothing about where he was! He was helpless in determining his own fate. (We know from the Scripture that he was later beheaded by Herod.) Yet he knew if he could get a message to the Lord an answer would be forthcoming. And it was!

Such a search is always rewarded. The heart that seeks after God will find Him, for "they that seek the Lord shall not want any good thing" (Psalms 34:10, KJV). Look at the reassuring proof the Lord sent back to John: "Go and show John *again* those things which ye do hear and see" (Matthew 11:4, KJV). No answer is more clearly defined than the one confirmed in our hearts by Him.

John was not unlike us! His doubts were perfectly human ones. Jesus never called him a weakling, never berated him. Nor did He look upon John as a doubting, cringing, disgruntled or faithless follower because he sought a reaffirmation of who Jesus was.

Instead, the Lord reaffirmed John. He called him a prophet. "A prophet...and more than a prophet...among them that are born of women there hath not come a greater than John the Baptist" (Matthew 11:9-11, KJV). God never condemns us for our honest doubts. He does challenge us to bring them to His feet, to Calvary.

You may be where the apostle was, struggling with life, trapped in the prison of your doubts, isolated and troubled with the unknowns of your future. But right there in the place of your doubting imprisonment, the Lord will touch you. He will touch you where you hurt and turn your doubts to belief.

CONTACT POINT

READ: Matthew 11:4-14; Luke 7:19-23

1. Define what you feel was the cause of John's question to Jesus.

a.

b.

c.

2. Do any of the above reasons ever apply to you personally?

3. List three reasons, or causes, that might have contributed to an area of doubt in your life. (past or present)

4. What three things do you think Jesus was telling John in His answer to him?

5. How can you apply to your own life the principles Jesus used in dealing with John? (Matthew 11:4-6)

APPLIED LEARNING

1. If you can remember a time in your life when God helped you during a doubting moment, write it out.

2. Find someone you think is discouraged and share your Christian testimony with that person.

3. Jot down the date of answered prayer in your Bible, on the calendar, or in your devotional notebook as a reminder to you in the future of what God has done for you in the past.

WHEN OUR DREAMS AND GOALS
BEGIN AT THE MASTER'S FEET THEY
PROVIDE A PATHWAY FOR GOD AND
MAN TO MEET.

5

Mend My Broken Dreams

We all know the value of goal-setting, of reaching for fulfillment and personal achievement. Motivational speakers, especially in the area of selling, all tell us about the importance of being goal-oriented. In fact, every success story I know is built around a dream — and a dreamer!

I love to watch people who are highly motivated. They inspire me. On the other hand, it saddens me to see those whose goals, ideals and dreams never seem to be actualized. Life can become a disappointment to those whose high hopes are thwarted by temporary setbacks. I say they are temporary because *broken dreams are not forever!*

When Our Dreams Are Put on Hold

Our broken dreams do not have to remain permanently shattered. There is a vast dif-

ference between the disappointment of delay
and the futility of never. Delay is the waiting
period between a God-given promise and the
time of its fruition. During those moments of
waiting our faith is tested most. We are not lost
from God's reach, but our messages don't seem
to be getting through to Him.

Recently as our spacecraft, the *Columbia,*
was launched into outer space, America stood
by to await the moments of L.O.S. (loss of
signal). During that brief time there was
nothing we could do but wait! This same thing
happens to us sometimes in our faith walk. We
lose signals—they don't seem to be getting
through to us. Our high-orbited dreams are
held in silence by the sway of the universe.

Daniel, the Old Testament prophet,
understood what it meant to pray and have the
answers to his prayers delayed. The angel who
later touched Daniel said, "Do not be afraid,
Daniel, for from the first day that you set your
heart on understanding this and on humbling
yourself before your God, your words were
heard, and I have come in response to your
words" (Daniel 10:12).

Because these delays come to us without ap-
parent reason, I call them *God's interruptions.*
During such times the heavens seem silent to
our cries. How we react to the situation reveals
more about our faith than about our dreams.

Patti had to wait for God to show Himself
to her in the fulfillment of her dreams. Don, her
husband, was active in a drug rehabilitation
program called Teen Challenge. While he was

speaking at our church one night, I glanced at Patti who was in the pew across from me. She had such a calm expression and serene appearance that I became curious. What was the secret of her glowing countenance?

Knowing our husbands were planning a day of relaxation on the golf course, I arranged to have her meet me for a light brunch the next morning. "Tell me about yourself," I began. "Do you have children?"

"We have three. Two of them are healthy, normal children, but our other child, Steve, was born with cerebral palsy. I don't talk much about it because it hurts too much. When I first heard the news of his problem, it left me in a state of mental shock. 'Things like this just don't happen to people like us,' I said. You see, I had never known anyone who had given birth to a handicapped child. Consequently, the thought of having anything other than a perfectly healthy child never entered in my mind.

"After he was born and we discovered the full extent of his handicap, I knew I had to deal with the emotional trauma. Certainly, I expected God to heal him. We, our family and friends, joined together in prayer. Each day we looked and hoped for the miracle that never came. As I waited, there were times I found myself withdrawing from life – even from God. I cannot say I was angry with God; I just didn't understand my broken dreams."

The tea I was sipping lost its flavor as I looked into the eyes of a mother whose dreams were delayed. I remembered the hurts I had felt from my own sister's retardation. Recalling some of the cruel glances, jibes of mockery and thoughtless comments that had hurt me, I hoped that Patti might be spared some of the agony. My heart ached for her!

She knew she would never see her child run in a marathon race, compete in a basketball tournament, or play pro football. But she couldn't give up! She had determined to cling to her belief that God had a plan for Steve.

I didn't see my friend, Patti, for years after that. We met again just a few months ago. She had the same clear-cut transparent glow about her countenance as before. I inquired about Steve, and she said she would write me the story. Her letter reached my desk a few days later.

"I remember times when Steve was growing up and how hard they were for all of us. There was one time that was most difficult for both Steve and me. We were sitting together inside the house looking out the sliding glass door, where the other children were playing. Rarely did Steve talk about his feelings. When he did talk about them I knew he was really hurting. He turned to me on that day and said, 'If only I could play, too!' His words literally broke my heart. I had to leave the room. . . .

"Steve is turning 20 now. He has learned to walk with a cane. Even though it has been difficult for him, we are proud of his academic record. In spite of his impaired speech and lack of motor control, he has adjusted to the classroom quite well. We are proud of him and the goals he has set for himself. One such goal is to finish high school. He will realize that dream when he graduates with the class of 1983.

"He has accepted Christ as his personal Saviour and has a dynamic testimony of faith. We take great pride in his achievements and in his persistence in maintaining his kind and loving personality."

As I read her letter I kept saying to myself, *This can't be all of the story. What have their broken dreams taught Don and Patti, and why are they able to be so serene?*

My questions were answered in a note from Don. It was attached with a postscript to Patti's letter. Don listed a series of lessons they had learned from the events that had transpired in their lives as they searched for answers to their son's problem. He summed those lessons up rather succinctly in the seven points listed below:

1. We learned to trust the sovereignty of God (Romans 8:28).
2. We became increasingly aware of God's constant love (Psalms 94:14).
3. The fact of God's sufficiency and grace was very real (2 Corinthians 12:9).
4. We learned to feel empathy and sympathy toward others (1 John 3:17).
5. Our work among criminals and drug addicts helped us understand that spiritual handicaps are worse than physical ones (Matthew 10:28).
6. Because of our need to depend upon Christ for daily strength, we "grew up

in Him" at a faster pace (Ephesians
4:15).
7. We learned to trust God more and question Him less (Ephesians 1:11).

When Don talked to me later, he mentioned
a discussion he had had with Dave Wilkerson.
Dave was the founder of Teen Challenge and
had experienced his own kind of broken
dreams. His wife had undergone surgery and
the reports were not good. Opposition was coming to him from all sides. Sharing with Don,
Mr. Wilkerson offered some guidelines from his
own life of trusting God:
"There are specific promises in God's Word
about healing, and there are other references
that deal with the sovereignty of God.
Sometimes His sovereign grace overrules a
specific promise at a particular time. We must
let Him be God of the whole of our lives. There
comes a time when we must quit trying to put
pressure on God to do something just for the
purpose of satisfying our mental inquiries.
God's purpose must be lived through us!"

Living in the Face of Difficulty

What about those people who must go on in
spite of their difficulty? Are they less spiritual
than others? No! Some of our greatest heroes
of faith worked for God in spite of their
handicaps.
Consider Fannie Crosby, who in her blindness
gave us songs like "Amazing Grace"; and Helen
Keller, who, with her multiplicity of physical

handicaps, was able to make history by what she did. She, who could neither hear nor see, turned the world of the non-hearing into a kaleidoscope of learning.

Sometimes it takes a greater degree of courage for some people just to live, than it does for others of us — who claim so much faith — to do what little we do. In my own life I have found this to be true. Living through the storms of my life called for courage and faith that demanded I trust God, even when I could see no miracle of deliverance forthcoming.

Our ideas of faith are often clouded or misguided by some current philosophy. Some views say we should believe God for a kind of divine utopia, while other views are prone to assign Him the tasks of playing quarterback and of making all the plays.

I observed this attitude one day as I walked out of the classroom where I had been teaching a weekly class of young marrieds from all denominations. I overheard one of the ladies say, "Praise the Lord," and I turned to see who had spoken. Other members of the class were rushing to the parking lot. A teenager had fallen off his bicycle and was lying on the pavement. The woman standing nearby was praising the Lord for the boy's broken leg. When I inquired about her strange reaction, she promptly quoted Romans 8:28: "For we know that all things work together for good to them that love God" (KJV).

What the lady did not understand is that the

verb *work* has a dual meaning. Finis Dake, the
Bible commentator, says the original Greek
sunergeo indicates that not only are all things
working, but as they are, God is also at work
in our behalf.[1] I like that explanation because
it helps me understand that God, who has
worked for me in the past, is presently at *work*
in me, and that He will continue to *work* on my
behalf. The progressive working of God brings
my life into a total perspective.

This changes the emphasis from an immediate action of a single event—one that
might be overwhelming to me if seen by
itself—into the blending of the whole of my
Christian experience. It is in that ongoing action that the completeness of design and struc-
ture is realized. Until I can fully understand
this, I may not be able to appreciate a spiritual
weaving process that is taking place in me; nor
will I be able to yield myself to the moving of
the shuttle that weaves those patterns. Recently I ran across the lines of a poem that has reinforced my thinking on this matter:

THE WEAVER
My life is but a weaving
  Between my Lord and me.
I cannot choose the colors
  He worketh steadily.

Ofttimes he weaveth sorrow
  And I in foolish pride,
Forget He sees the upper
  And I the underside.

Not until the loom is silent
  And the shuttles cease to fly,
Shall God unroll the canvas
  And explain the reasons why.

The dark threads are as needful
  In the Weaver's skillful hand
As the threads of gold and silver
  In the pattern He has planned.

                            Grant Tolfax Tullar

(Reprinted from tract #53, published by Faith, Prayer and Tract
League, Grand Rapids, Michigan.)

Living Dreams and Dying Egos

The apostle Paul was a dreamer, a man of great goals. He had hopes that were high and noble ones. Yet, he never reached the height of his fullest ambitions — at least, not in this life. Paul's hopes were not based in selfish ambitions either; they were Kingdom-oriented.

His greatest desire was to go to Spain to spread the gospel to the furthermost point of the Roman Empire. He didn't want to go there on a pleasure trip. He wanted to go because he knew men like Seneca, the Roman Senator, and Lucian the poet, lived there. Reaching those men with the gospel would provide him with the greatest vantage point of his entire ministry. Yet, as noble as those desires were, I find no place recorded in the scripture where Paul ever reached Spain.

The apostle Paul's life ended in a Roman cell. Or did it? No, God took his noble desire and transported it into an even more worthy cause. As a result of the apostle's life and influence, his message went far beyond his dreams. It was because he was willing to submit himself and to relinquish his immediate dream to a higher call. His was a dream that rested in the will of God. The beautiful part about this man's character is that he was able to do so without rancor or bitterness toward God and people. No wonder he could come to the dying hours of his life and say, "I have fought the good fight, I have finished the course, I have kept the faith" (2 Timothy 4:7).

We may be injured and our dreams delayed, but we do not have to be stockpiled! The secret is found as we hang our dreams upon the cross. When we put them there, the focus of our dreams moves from us to Calvary. It is then, and only then, that we are able to pray as Jesus did, "Yet not as I will, but as Thou wilt" (Matthew 26:39). Whatever personal goals we may have, they can be pursued with diligence, as long as we keep them attached to the cross of God's divine plan. For that reason I encourage you to hang onto your dreams.

Hang On To Your Dreams When You Are Tempted To Give Up

There was an Old Testament youth by the name of Joseph who was called "a dreamer." You remember the story of his early life, of his being sold into slavery by his own brothers, Joseph was later cast into prison because of his moral principles. Yet he never abandoned his dreams. I believe there were two reasons for the young man's courage. First, *he did not wait until the time of crisis in his life to set his moral and spiritual standards.* They had been established long before he was sold into Egypt. They surfaced when he was tempted by Potiphar's wife. The lies of this woman caused him imprisonment, isolation, disappointment, and prolonged waiting—but those things did not alter his character or personality. They did not change him from the man he was.

Second, *Joseph did not give up his dreams.* He knew they were God-given. There are times when we, like Joseph, must hang on to our personal goals and dreams when we think they are slipping from us. Even when our head says, *No, things will never develop for my good,* our faith in God can reply, *Yes, it can and it will, because of WHO GOD IS!*

Hang On To Your Dreams When It Would Be Easy to Give Up

Bruce Lietzke, a pro golfer, won a tournament because he refused to give up. He played his first round of golf that day in great pain. A torn stomach muscle was affecting his back swing, and he decided to drop out of the game. His family and friends were called together and he planned to break the news to them first.

They all met at an oriental restaurant. But then Bruce determined he would say nothing about his plan to quit, nor would he mention the excruciating pain. Instead, he braced himself, went back out and won the Tucson Open Tournament.

Hang On To Your Dreams When You Think God and People Have Forgotten You

We all know people who could help us if they would. Sometimes our friends may arbitrarily choose not to do so. Their choice is not against us personally. Perhaps those who could help us are caught up in their own needs and are oblivious to ours. Sometimes they choose to react out of their own personal likes and dislikes.

Then, too, there are always those who might feel threatened by a dreamer, a goal setter. Because of those psychological hangups, they are afraid to give us the opportunity to excel.

And there might be another reason for not finding the support we need and expect from others. *It could be that God wants us to depend solely upon Him!* That is how God dealt with me. While struggling to get my first book on the market, I met with some disappointing moments. Those friends I thought would help me most showed the least interest in my work.

Peoples' responses bothered me a great deal. One day while praying I was reminded of a verse in Psalms. "For promotion cometh neither from the east, nor from the west, nor from the south. But God is the judge: he putteth down one, and setteth up another" (Psalms 75:6, 7, KJV).

After reading it I knew that God was the one who would have to be my source. He would be the one in whom I would trust. I have found that God will, and does, take care of me! Sometimes He does it in very unusual ways and through the least likely persons. In most cases, He works through people other than those from whom we expected the help to come to us.

Hang On To Your Dreams When You Feel Life is Passing You By

It is never too late to dream. Cling to your dreams even when you think life is unfair and people are passing you by. A lovely black lady from Hanford, California, is an example of what I call tenacity! She had not had the privilege of an education. After she was more than 70 years old, she decided to go to school. She later graduated from the local high school and went on to enter college. The woman did not quit until she had earned her B.A. degree.

Caleb, of the Old Testament, is another person who refused to give up his dreams. He would not abandon them because of age nor for any other reason. When he went with the other spies to view the land of Canaan, he saw things none of the younger men saw. A dream was born within him! He liked what he saw and wanted to live in the hills of Hebron. That mountainous area became his dreamland. Yet he had to wait, a victim of the choices of other people, for 40 years before his dream was actualized. He never gave up, and when the time came, he reminded Joshua of his promised land:

"Behold, the Lord has let me live, just as He spoke, these forty-five years, and from the time that the Lord spoke this word to Moses, when Israel walked in the wilderness; and now, behold I am eighty-five years old today. I am still as strong today as I was in the day Moses sent me" (Joshua 14:10, 11).

Caleb got that mountain!

Delayed dreams are often difficult because they leave so much time for doubting. You may be tempted to doubt yourself, to become bitter with those who thwart those dreams, and to give up too soon. It is true that sometimes other people, and their lack of understanding our dreams, may prolong the fulfillment of them. Yet, no person or circumstance can withhold God's blessing from our lives! What we fail to grasp sometimes is that the combination of timing and opportunity must come together. My experience has been that within the providential framework of God's plan, He will be true to His promises to us!

CONTACT POINT

READ: Psalms 57:7; Luke 14:28

1. What does the psalmist mean by a "steadfast heart"?

2. What does Luke 14:28 say to you personally?

3. Can you recall an unfulfilled dream in your life? Were you disappointed by it? Did you

discover later that had the incident occurred it would not have been in your best interest?

a. What did you learn by it?

b. How did you react toward it at the time?

c. Have you remembered to give the Lord thanks for knowing what was best for you?

4. How many different goals/dreams are you trying to reach at this very time? What effect is this having on your spiritual self?

5. Can you, at this time, bring your goals/dreams to the Lord and pray, "Not as I will, but according to Your will"?

APPLIED LEARNING

1. Write out Philippians 4:13 and attach it to something near you where you will see it often.

2. Repeat the verse to yourself verbally, everytime you see it, for the next two weeks.

[1]*Dake Bible*, Lawrenceville, Ga: Dake Bible Sales, Inc., 1961, p. 167.

THE DOOR OF FORGIVENESS SWINGS
FROM TWO HINGES: THE NEED TO BE
FORGIVEN AND THE NEED TO
FORGIVE.

6

Forgive Me as I Forgive

Gene and Karla were members of my Practical
Christian Living Class. After experiencing a
communication problem in their marriage, they
shared what they had learned through the
difficulty.

"I came from a family with all girls in the
house," Karla explained. "My mother was an
immaculate housekeeper. Naturally, I
developed the same attitude toward my home.
Gene, my husband, came from an altogether
different set of circumstances."

"That's right," Gene said. "In our house we
enjoyed living. It was a place to eat, to have
a good time, and to bring all our friends."

Karla chimed in, "When we went to buy furniture, I wanted a coffee table to enhance the
looks of our living room."

"I felt the only reason for having a coffee
table was for me to put my feet on," Gene

replied. They felt each was misunderstanding the other, and conflicts increased. Gene explained why. "We were coming from divergent backgrounds and points of reference. I was thinking of the only way I thought a coffee table was to be used. My wife was remembering how neatly her mother had kept theirs. Each of us had to stop and listen to what the other was saying. We not only had to listen — we had to forgive. We were unable to do that until we took time to understand each other."

Fortunately, Gene and Karla were able to resolve their problem in an objective manner. Most of us are often unable to do so. Many times what we think is being said and what people are saying are two different messages. When this happens a problem develops in our relationships. In most cases there is the need for understanding and forgiveness. It is forgiveness we need, but we are usually afraid to admit it!

Admitting to a Problem Means Dealing With It

When we are afraid to admit there is a problem, we have to skirt the issue in many ways. We may harbor resentment, never giving the other person a chance to make amends. Years later, or maybe sooner, our attitude will be revealed to us through some incident that reminds us. I learned this the hard way!

Claude and I had just moved into our new condominium. Of course, I was particular about each item of furniture and where it should be placed. Since there was no dining room chandelier, I selected one at the store. It was a hand-painted porcelain fixture, and I waited for two years before making the special purchase. It was an exciting day for me when I returned home with the lamp. I could hardly wait for my husband to hang it for me.

I insisted it must be hung right then, forgetting it was Super Bowl weekend. A sports fan, Claude did not want to hang the chandelier that day. Because of my insistence, he agreed to work on the project during half-time and the commercial breaks. After assembling all of the tools, the two of us proceeded on the minute-by-minute work plan.

We were standing on chairs working together; I was holding the equipment, he the chandelier. I reached to hand him the painted base that was to have been attached to the ceiling. Instead, the piece slipped through his hands and fell shattering against the living room table.

I could not understand how he could have been so careless with something that meant that much to me. The porcelain piece would have to be replaced with an ordinary metal attachment, and I was deeply disappointed!

Neither of us talked about it, other than his apology for having dropped it. Secretly I wondered, *Did he really know how much that light meant to me?*

Time taught me the lesson. Months later when our daughter Jan, moved to Scottsdale, Arizona, I went over to assist her in the move.

When we had her house in order, I packed and was ready to leave for home. Before I left we decided to assemble her new lamp. As I handed her the heavy metal ornament that held the lamp shade to its base, I dropped the piece. It fell bouncing across the top of her new end table, causing a bad dent in the highly polished wood. *How could I have been so clumsy?* I thought. Then I remembered the other incident! And I understood that not only did I need to forgive, but, also needed the same forgiveness. *Life is an echo.* Whatever we put into the lives of others will come back into our own. For when we cease to forgive, we are no longer forgiven. *Forgiveness is God's absolution and our opportunity to begin again — to rebuild what is torn down and to mend what is broken!*

We will never know God's forgiveness until we have faced our need of forgiveness from Him and others. Nor will we understand the loving qualities of our heavenly Father until we have learned something of His forgiving nature. If we harbor an unforgiving attitude, we close the door of blessing and we damage ourselves.

Sonja, a woman I once knew, taught me the tragedy of what happens in the life of one who refuses to forgive. When I visited her, I discovered a woman who was ill both physically and spiritually. A bitter woman who hated life and people, she was dying. I soon realized that if anyone had a right to be bitter, she certainly did.

"I have always led people to believe I had no relatives. Let me explain something to you. You can see I have no one to care for me. It is not because I have no family that I lie here dying alone. My sister, Eleanor, lives within a few miles of here. We have not seen each other for years. She would come to see me, but I cannot bear to see her face.

"Eleanor chose to remain unmarried, but I married at a very early age. After many years, my husband and I discovered I was unable to bear children. Eleanor began carrying on an affair with my husband. She bore a son by him. I took the child right after his birth and raised him as my own. There was no contact between Eleanor and me for many years. Then when the child was a teenager, she reentered my life. She turned my 'son' against me, and he moved in with her. I have lived alone in my sorrow all these years without seeing either of them."

While she was speaking I thought of the times she had lashed out against others in our church. Her anger was venomous, and she had repeatedly spat it out against anyone who dared to disagree with her. I knew about some of the times when she had needed and received forgiveness from her pastor and friends. Yet she was refusing to forgive!

I agreed that she had every reason to feel hurt, neglected and forgotten. I knew the situation demanded more grace than she could give. But I also knew her hurt would never go away without forgiveness. If emotional and spiritual

healing were ever to come to Sonja, she would
have to take the initiative in reconciliation.

Who Takes The Initiative In Forgiveness?

God always takes the initiative in drawing
us toward Him. Since He is our example, we
need to remember His principle. How often we
hear the statement, "I didn't do anything, and
I won't ask forgiveness for something I did not
do." Jesus reverses this perspective. He says,
"If therefore you...remember that your brother
has something against you...go your way; first
be reconciled to your brother" (Matthew 5:23,
24). This deals with both the offender and the
offended. Equal responsibility rests upon the
two of them to deal with the matter. Reconciliation must be started by the one who feels offended if it is not initiated by the offender. That
does not sound fair does it?

There must be a reason for this approach. As
I think about this, I ask myself three questions:
*Did Christ demand the action because the
other person might not have been aware that
they offended the first one? Was He giving the
supreme example of what is demanded in Christian conduct? Could it have been that He
wanted to leave no loopholes, no excuses for
broken relationships?* Because Christ came to
be peace between man and man and between
man and God (Ephesians 2:14-16), I believe all
three questions require an affirmative reply.
When Jesus prayed, "Father forgive them for
they know not what they do," He assumed the
position of the one who had offended the

Father. In so doing He became the mediator and initiated reconciliation.

It isn't easy to be the one to initiate reconciliation, especially if we are the ones who are seeking forgiveness. There is always the tendency to want to absolve ourselves of wrongdoing. To ease our own conscience, we might have a tendency to want the offender to bear an undue amount of guilt. It is vital when we approach another for forgiveness that we never lay a transferred load upon the person from whom we seek that forgiveness.

I never realized how important that was until the following incident occurred in my life. I was seated on the front row of the church waiting to be introduced as the Retreat speaker. Beside me sat a lady whom I had not met prior to that day. Just as I was about to step onto the platform she handed me this note:

"Ruthe, will you forgive me? I didn't like you when I met you."

My mind went into orbit. *What had I done to her? Why didn't she like me?* Of course, I was willing to forgive her, but it left me bewildered. No doubt her motive was right, but her approach was untimely. Up to that point the matter had been a secret between her and God, and in consideration for the total effect it would have on the ministry that night, it might have been better if she had prayed about it, allowing God to forgive her rather than asking me. If we have a genuine desire to do what is right,

we will want to do it in a way that will bring
ultimate blessing to the offending party.

The Attitude Of Forgiveness

Forgiveness is more than an attitude, it is an
act of our will. We decide whether we are going to forgive or not. Sometimes when we
choose to do so, we can be smug and take on
a superpious air; especially when someone
comes to us to apologize. It is as if we are saying, "Well, it's about time!"

God never lets me get by with that attitude.
One day while walking down a street in Tulsa,
Oklahoma, I heard someone calling me.

"Lady, lady! Are you Ruthe White? Was your
maiden name Carter, and did you once live in
Tupelo, Oklahoma?"

I answered "yes" to all the woman's questions.

"Forgive me," she said. "I have wanted to see
you for many years. When I read in the
newspaper that you were speaking in our city,
I determined that I would see you. Remember
when we all went to school together, you, your
brothers and me?"

"Yes, I remember!" She had never been kind
to us, and I felt ruffled.

"I often made fun of you and your family,
especially your mentally retarded sister. I have
accepted Jesus — that same Jesus your family
talked with me about. He has forgiven me of
my sins, but all these years, in growing up, I
have hated myself for what I did to you during my teen years. Please, forgive me!"

My first reaction was to retort, "You *were* a

bigot, weren't you?" But then I knew it was she who had the Christ-like spirit, not I. The carnal, human side of me wanted to lay more guilt upon her, to make her suffer for what she had done to me. At the same time, as I became willing to forgive, I knew I could never gloat over having been right all of the time. I forgave her, and even as she walked away, I knew there was healing in forgiving.

How Many Times Do We Forgive?

When Peter, the disciple, asked the Lord how many times to forgive, he was not unwilling to forgive; he just wanted to know what the limits were. The rabbis could have answered his inquiry, as they had done many times before, by referring to their legalistic understanding of the Old Testament Law. They had concluded, through their interpretation of the Law, that one was to forgive a maximum of three times, no more (Amos 1:3; 2:6). Somehow, what the Jewish leaders were saying and what Jesus was teaching seemed different.

Impulsive, boastful Peter was willing to raise that number from three to seven. Jesus, in turn, clearly stated the unlimited measure of forgiveness. He spoke not of seven times, but seventy times seven (Matthew 18:21, 22). What a contrast to the vengeful attitude that is reflected in the sinful nature of man! Man's limited forgiveness is measured against the limitless forgiveness of God.

Under the penalty of the law we would have been cut off for one mistake, not three.

Under grace our erring nature finds forgiveness repeated in the nature of God. What one of us does not need to return to Calvary again and again?

The Scope Of God's Forgiveness

But there is more to God's forgiving nature than quantity. The wideness of His mercy covers more than we can comprehend. Pastor George Greg, a friend of ours, had this to say about the scope of God's forgiveness:

> "In my opinion, forgiveness is the most single theme in the Word of God. It is essential that believers understand the basis of that forgiveness, and vital to understand the completeness of God's forgiveness.
>
> "We are prone to believe that God can forgive almost everything. Contained within the walls of the almost, there is a disturbing strain of unforgiveness. We sometimes cannot forgive ourselves of a mistake, and we will not allow God to forgive us because we don't believe He will!"

Without question there is, or was, an enormous debt of sin that rested upon each of us. It is a debt no one can fully pay. Although we know we need to be released from it, somehow, there is the feeling that some things are harder for God to forgive than others. Let us never forget that as we come to Christ Jesus *all* debts are cancelled, forgiven. The basis of that work rests upon the declaration of God's forgiving nature. It does not come because I have earned special brownie points for being good.

Forgiveness rests solely upon the merits of His grace (Ephesians 2:8, 9).

There is Finality in The Act of God's Forgiveness

Once we have come to God with our need to be forgiven, we must understand the scope of His forgiveness and the finality of the act. Once a sin is confessed it is never worth our remembering again. We should not allow ourselves to become victims of Satan's attempts to throw our guilt back at us. Once our sins are forgiven they are just as forgiven as they will ever be, and just as forgiven as they need to be!

Yet some of us do quite well in dredging up the skeletons of our past. Skillfully we attempt to drape them in coverings of self-righteousness. Or we go to the other extreme. We keep digging at the shallowness of our human nature, refusing to accept God's depth of forgiveness. At the same time, Satan, who is our accuser, will take our sensitive, tender hearts and rail against our consciences with accusations (Revelation 12:10). We need to be aware of his tactics!

Three things happen when we begin to accept God's forgiving nature. *One, we never again need to be trapped by self-condemnation.* "For God did not send His Son into the world to judge the world, but that the world should be saved through Him" (John 3:17). *Two, Satan cannot accuse us unjustly before God, because God's Son, Jesus, stands as our intercessor.* "He is able to save forever those who draw near to God through him, since He always lives to make intercession for them" (Hebrews 7:25). *Three, no longer do we have to feel intimidated by our personal inadequacies.* Paul, the apostle said, "When I am weak, then I am strong" (2 Corinthians 12:10).

Out of our weakness comes strength, forgiveness, and healing!

CONTACT POINT

READ: Matthew 6:5-15; Mark 3:28; 2 Corinthians 2:7; Ephesians 4:3; Colossians 3:13; Luke 15:11-32.

1. How can we learn about God by studying His forgiving nature?

2. In the story of the prodigal son, what three aspects of love are shown by the father, toward his son.

a.

b.

c.

3. How is the story of the prodigal son related to God our heavenly Father?

4. Is forgiveness a Christian command, or is it a free choice of the will? Can it be both? If so, how?

5. How does our forgiveness rest upon our own willingness to forgive others? Does it have any relationship to our own salvation? How?

APPLIED LEARNING

Will you agree to do these three things?

1. Ask yourself if you have an unforgiving spirit. If so, to whom is it directed?

2. Pray for that person, or persons, each day for 30 days.

3. Ask God to show you how to react to the situation as He would react. Be honest with Him about how you feel.

PART III

Send Me

TOUCH ME AGAIN, LORD

Touch me, Lord,
That I might see,
  The weakness of my humanity.

Touch me again, Lord,
And cause me to see,
Your *divine plan* at work in me.

ONLY GOD CAN DECLARE OUR
RIGHTEOUSNESS. WE WILL NEVER
"GET GOOD ENOUGH" TO EARN IT.

7

To Tell Others Christ Is Their Righteousness

"Take it off, sister."

"No, put it on."

Some people thought I should take off my wedding band. Others felt I should wear it. I seemed to be either too worldly to be righteous or too righteous to be worldly. I could never decide which! But when I returned to our travel trailer from church and found Claude disassembling the television antenna, I suspected things were really bad.

"What on earth are you doing?" I inquired.

"Taking down the rabbit ears," he replied. "The people in this church think we are evil because we have a TV."

"Well, I guess we can do anything once," I muttered. "But I am sure glad we're going to be here for only two weeks; this speaking jaunt is killing me!"

Before the two weeks were up we had found ways of skirting the television issue. Each night, after we thought the more saintly saints had retired, Claude would climb onto our travel unit and reconnect the fork-toothed receptor. Before retiring, we would lower the antenna again. Raising and lowering the apparatus was unpleasant at first; then it became humorous. But dealing with Sister Gertrude was s-o-m-e-thing else!

Gertrude came into the church every night and took her seat right up front. After tucking her long dress around her ankles, she would then fold her arms across her buxom torso and with a sullen stare, look my husband right in the eye. She never changed her expression from the time he introduced his message until it was finished. Her belligerent attitude made me feel she didn't care much for his preaching. I knew she didn't like *me* when she approached me one night after the service.

"Your hair offends me, them curls on top of your head ain't godly, and don't you know God's righteousness demands holiness?"

She blurted out the statement in one long and hurried breath. After making her spiel she turned on her heel and headed for the door. The tight-fisted bun, which held her mousey-grey hair in place, seemed to bounce back at me as she stomped out.

By this time I had begun to feel like an escalator moving in two directions at once, and my heart felt like it was in a vice—one that was being tightened more and more. I knew it was time for me to talk to God about the situation:

"God, do I *have* to look and act like her to be holy? You know I love You, but—I can't stand *her!* If she is like You, then I *am* confused. I really want to serve You. I have always believed Your Word about the beauty of Your holiness. That is what I want—I want to know the magnificence of Your beauty. I am willing to do anything *You* ask me to. Amen.

P.S. Please, God. Don't make me look like Sister Gertrude!"

As a young minister's wife, I soon discovered that there were Gertrudes all over the world who would put legalistic demands upon me *if I let them*. It was enlightening to learn that each geographic location had its own set of cultural mores and traditions, and the church was not exempt. The criteria for holiness changed with each locale! For instance, in some parts of the nation there were those believers who would not drink a Coca Cola. A Pepsi, yes—*if* they didn't drink it from a bottle!

Those traditional demands for conformity were little more than legalism. They had nothing to do with God's righteousness, nor mine! The people who were placing those demands upon me were asking me *to perform and conform to man's standards*. The more I tried to please them, the more the emphasis was being shifted from the acceptance of Christ's finished work to the arduous task of finding man's approval. I found myself running headlong into the question, *When will I ever get good enough to be righteous?*

Eventually, after years of my struggling with this issue, God opened my eyes. He showed me I was trying to live up to criteria set by human reasoning and meant to satisfy human demands. That could not be!

You and I will never "get good enough" to obtain righteousness because it is the result of God's work done for us. Salvation and righteousness are not dependent upon what we have done to earn it. Likewise, we are not lost because of our sin. If we are lost, it is because we have not repented of our sins and accepted the covering of His cleansing which is provided through Jesus. We do not rid ourselves of sin in order to come to God. We come to Him and He rids us of sin! This moves the focus away from us and our sinful nature to the Lord Jesus who is, and forever seeks to be, our righteousness!

What a tragedy when someone within the church body feels victimized by, or trapped into, an attitude of legalism. Aletha, a woman from Missouri, talked with me about how her son was caught in such a framework of thinking.

"My son is recently divorced. He knows the position of the church on that issue. Because of his divorced situation, and knowing the feeling of some in the church, he has begun to feel himself outside the scope of God's righteousness. After months of isolation and living with his hurt, he decided to come back to the church. He went to the pastor and asked, 'Reverend, will you just *let me* attend the meetings?' The pastor grudgingly obliged."

I wonder, *Did the man feel he was no longer eligible for God's righteousness? If so, who was responsible?*

Jeane, a lady with three marriages behind her and three sets of children from those marriages, came to one of my retreats. Because of her early life she had developed an inferiority complex. After observing her, I realized she was having problems relating with the other women. Her behavior was sometimes loud and boisterous; her clothing was gaudy — almost ostentatious, and extreme in style. Instead of her being withdrawn because of her poor self-image, she was reacting to people aggressively. The women there were tolerating her but not showing much Christian love.

I was pleased when she came to me, but her story grieved me.

"Mother was pregnant with me when she got married. She divorced my father shortly after my birth. Both my parents abandoned me, and I was left to the order of the courts. I was placed in one foster home after another.

"Dad remarried when I was about six. He and my new stepmother took me in. They put a roof over my head, but they didn't show me any love. One night when I was twelve, I overheard them arguing about me. I sneaked out of the bedroom window and ran away. While walking down a dark street, I was spotted by a carload of five men who stopped and picked me up. They took me to an old motel where they took turns raping me. Then they tied me to a bedpost and left me in the motel room alone. I was there for three days and nights. Finally, after the third day I was able to break loose and make a getaway. I walked across town and back home. My father was so upset at me for running away from our family that he beat me.

"During the years that followed I was shifted from one detention home to another. By the time I was 16 I was considered an incorrigible delinquent.

"Look at me. I am now in my 40's, trying to put my life together. I know nothing but rejection, and I feel it strongly right here among these church women. Tell me, Ruthe, will I ever get good enough for God to love me? Can I expect His righteousness to cover my sins?"

I reminded Jeane that His covering knows no boundaries. She had already accepted Christ as her Saviour, but found it difficult to grasp His forgiving nature. She had been led to believe His atonement did not avail for her, and that if she suffered enough through her guilt, a purging element would evolve from the punitive agony of her past. God's righteousness was an unsolved mystery to her!

Anytime we do not understand something, that object becomes an obscure uncertainty. Often the image of our worth is lost in the distorted, abstract and confusing demands of *what we think God requires.*

Such conditioning makes it difficult to believe a Holy God can accept fallen man. The idea of His *unreachability* is often reinforced by the church. Consciously or not, we have been guilty of wanting people to do penance, to suffer, to abstain from evil and to get good enough for God to accept them. We assure them if they will meet the requirements we have set forth, they will arrive at some nebulous state of holiness.

Some of us, in our great desire to serve God, are willing to follow those legalistic demands, but there are others who become discouraged and give up. While we may not say so, our conduct sometimes makes people feel their sin was, or is, worse than ours. We, in effect, are trying to put those people back under the Old Testament law instead of teaching them about God's grace.

Mosaic law required lepers (who in Scripture often typified sinners) to remain outside the walls of the city and to cry, "Unclean, unclean!" They were to touch no one and no one was to touch them. Yet, it is interesting to see how Jesus approached those untouchables.

"And behold, a leper came to Him and bowed down to Him, saying, 'Lord, if you are willing, You can make me *clean.*' And *He stretched out His hand and touched him, saying, 'I am willing; be cleansed'*" (Matthew 8:2, 3, italics added).

Here is a picture of the *immaculate one,* in whom rests the purity and holiness of God, reaching out to touch the dreadful defilement of a leprous man.

He caused the *untouchable* to be *touchable!*

When Will I Get Righteous Enough to Become Good?

If you and I don't try to get good enough to come to God, we may feel instead that God is incomprehensible and that His demands for perfection are greater than we can ever attain. We may try to behave righteously enough to become good – so good that we will never make a mistake. One approach is as devastating as the other, for they are two sides of the same coin. The Mosaic law was so strict no one could adhere to it. It was intended to show man the futility of his efforts to save himself. The law was the schoolmaster or tutor, the purpose of which was to point men to Christ. "Therefore the Law has become our tutor to lead us to Christ, that we may be justified by faith" (Galatians 3:24).

The law of Moses could only point out man's sin. It could not bring deliverance from the sin. If I have fallen into a well and can't get out, I don't want someone standing by to tell me where I am. I want that person to throw me a rope and help me get out. I already know the penalty of my error, and I know I am drowning! At that point I am looking for a deliverer! Our deliverer is Jesus Christ.

How Righteous Is Righteous?

Once we have accepted Christ, our righteousness is based not in us, but *Him*. When God forgives, He imputes (takes into account, or metaphorically, puts down to a person's account) His own righteousness. "Therefore by the deeds of the law there shall no flesh be justified in his sight; for by the law is the knowledge of sin.

"But now the righteousness of God without the law is manifested, being witnessed by the law and the prophets . . . For all have sinned and come short of the glory of God; being justified freely by His grace through the redemption that is in Christ Jesus" (Romans 3:20-24, KJV).

"But to him that worketh not, but believeth on him that justifieth the ungodly, his faith is counted for righteousness. Even as David also describeth the blessedness of the man, unto whom God *imputeth righteousness without works*" (Romans 4:5-6, KJV).

So the quality of God's righteousness remains the same. It is not diminished as it passes from God to us, and that makes us as righteous as *we can be or need to be!* Once we understand this concept, we can be free of the bondage to human demands and human standards. Like graduates from high school, we can use the principles we have learned without being bound to the teacher — to the Old Testament law. When we trust Christ to be our righteousness, we can share with others the good news that they, too, can be free.

CONTACT POINT

READ: Hebrews 5:13; John 16:8-10; Matthew 5:6; Romans 3:25-27

1. Write out Webster's definition of righteousness.

2. According to Vine's Expository, the word *righteousness* literally means "rightwiseness."

a. Is it an attribute of God? Romans 3:5

b. How is righteousness given?

c. Is it attainable and how? Romans 4; Ephesians 6:14

3. How is God's righteousness made known to us? Romans 3:25

4. What is the scope of God's righteousness as recorded in Romans 3?

a. Past

b. Present

c. Future

5. What part does faith have in the application of God's righteousness toward us?

APPLIED LEARNING

1. List three things about Christ's death and Calvary that assures you of His righteousness.

2. What is meant by the Scripture, "hunger and thirst for righteousness" (Matthew 5:6)?

3. Once we have found Christ as Saviour, what demand does He place upon us for living? Romans 12:1, 2; 2 Timothy 3:15(KJV).

8

To Tell Others God Really Cares

Audrey Meir, song writer, choral director and author, tells this story: "I was the accompanist for a singer at a men's luncheon. The group of laymen, over-fed with beef and gravy, were not listening to what the older missionary speaker had to say. Fresh from the mission field, he was most anxious to communicate his message to them. Finally, after a desperate effort to relate and seemingly getting nowhere with the group, the missionary paused, broke into tears and said: 'What I really want to tell you is, it matters to Him about you.' I was so inspired by his statement, I took a pen from my purse and on the corner of the tablecloth where I was seated I scribbled the words to the song, 'It Matters to Him About You' [©Manna Music]."

We all need to feel someone cares about us. To admit to that need is to say we are human, earthy individuals who are capable of feeling—

and touching. We also want others to feel with us when we hurt and to touch our lives in a caring way.

Today people have to deal with situations which are unlike those known to any former generation. Until about 40 years ago it was the norm for family members to live and die within 25 miles of their birthplace. They knew nothing of mass transit systems, or the temporary lifestyle that is so common among us now. They never experienced the mobility of the modern day jet-setters. Our forefathers had support groups among their peers and roots within their neighborhoods. We lack that stability in our present-day society! No doubt that is one reason for the recent emphasis on re-establishing our family "roots."

Because of this impermanency of life patterns, it is easy to develop an impersonal approach to living. Somehow, the attitude becomes one of not needing others. Computerization, as good as it might be, has added to the situation by making problem-solving a one-person show. We can sit in our living rooms and push buttons as answers are spit back at us from behind the conclaves of mechanization. As a result, we sometimes tend to think of others as just another voice, a commodity, or a faceless number.

Numbers identify us. In a recent article, the *Fresno Bee* of Fresno, California, pointed this out:

"We are largely a collection of numbers. Once upon a time only convicts were numbered.

Spencer Nelson, publisher of a newsletter on credit cards, says that there are more than 586 million credit card types outstanding in the United States today. They average 5.1 pieces of plastic per American and predict that by the year 1985 it will have reached 8.4. Walter Cavanagh, a drug store manager from Santa Clara, California, holds the record of 897 cards."[1]

How easy it is to see ourselves — and others — as faceless, nameless, pieces of plastic. Not only so, but along with de-emphasis upon personhood, we fail to take time for developing relationships. Our children are growing up without knowing how to care, to feel, or to have empathy for others. They have been given transistors at the earliest possible age, encouraged to go to their private rooms, plug into their head sets, and live in a world of their own choosing. As adults we plug into our isolationism with tiny ear mikes as we jog through life. We listen in on what we want to and close the rest of the world out. As a result, this generation has become the most plugged-in, revved-up, tuned-out society in the history of the world.

In addition, the fast moving pace of the information explosion has added to the busy-ness of our lives. We are inundated with the process of change. So much data is being thrown at us we can no longer assimilate it, and we feel victimized by commercialism, materialism and sexism. Well-paid psychologists in the marketing media drain us of our emotional and spiritual resources. We want more things than we can possibly pay for. So we hammer along at life in our own isolated world of problems, trying to make a living, often forgetting that someone is longing to hear us say, "We care."

Gina, a young mother with four children, felt she could run her life without the aid of others. She once said to me, "I don't need the fellowship of other church women. I have my husband and children, and I am quite fulfilled in my role as mother and wife." A few years later that same woman began going through one tragedy after another. Illness, death and financial problems hit her all at once. She then came to understand how much it meant to know someone cared.

The need for caring knows no age limits or sociological boundaries. This fact was clearly shown in a recent movie entitled "The Untold Story." The film showed excerpts from the life and tragic death of the late actress, Marilyn Monroe. One statement came through clearly: She died wanting to feel loved, wanting to know someone cared for her and understood her!

Not only do we need understanding, we will do almost anything to get it. We are like the youngster who was asked by a visiting minister, "Sonny, why do you walk clear across town each Sunday to attend this church?"

The child looked up into the man's eyes and replied, "Sir, they love a fellar around here!"

We will go to almost any lengths to be near someone if we think they care, really care, about us. Yet, how easy it is for us to neglect to share with others the caring nature of God.

Melba Hudson was a self-effacing, efficient business lady. She was also a loving, caring person. I sat in the Sunday school class she was teaching week after week, not realizing how much she needed to know someone cared. At one time, over a period of several weeks, I felt an urgent need to pray for her. After mentioning her name in prayer I would go on about my daily activities, thinking I would call her later. After about two months the concern I had once felt for her began to diminish.

One day she told the class, "I have, over the past few weeks, walked through the darkest valley of my life. The thought kept coming to me, *no one cares. If only someone did, I could handle this problem so much easier.*"

I cannot tell you how I felt! I determined to meet with her for lunch during the coming week, so I could tell her that I had been praying for her and that I cared very much.

That opportunity never came! A freak accident at a railroad stop forced Melba's car into the path of an incoming train. She died without knowing someone cared. Since then I have made a point of sharing with people my love for them. Even if I am unaware of the specifics of an individual's needs, I can put feet to my prayers by dropping a note in the mail or by making a quick phone call. I don't need to know the details — God handles them.

God Cares And He Understands

Because God understands the cause of our pain, He is able to deal with the source of our problem. To grasp this truth is not enough; we must also appropriate His understanding and His promise to help. Kathi Bulman, a young woman from Apple Valley, California, learned this, and she wrote to tell me about her experience.

"I have always had a weight problem. When I first met you it was obvious, by the way I looked, that my eating was out of control. I was carrying 210 pounds on my five-foot-five frame and wearing a size 24 dress. My problem had begun when we moved to the desert. In a matter of days I went from being a successful career woman to a mother and housewife. I quickly lost all self-confidence as my identity was being absorbed into that of my family. Within a year and a half I gained over 60 pounds!

"Soon I was in the vicious cycle:

FEEL BAD – EAT – GUILT – FEEL BAD.

"I thought I was punishing my husband, Rick, and I blamed him for not stopping me from eating. I dared him to love me fat! Because of my weight I always was mistaken for being in my 40's when, in fact, I was only 27.

"During the retreat where you spoke, I found myself mentally blocking out what you were saying. It was like a blur to me. You see, a person who is totally wrapped up in herself misses a lot.

"When I asked you, 'Why won't God help me and do you think He understands my problem?' your answer knocked me off my feet. You turned to me and said, 'Yes, Kathi, God does understand. He knows you so well He wants to help you take responsibility for dealing with the real cause. You take the first step. Then God will help you because He cares for you.'

> "I came home from that retreat with a new excitement! It's been a year now and I have already lost 60 pounds. Thank you for helping me to know the loving and caring nature of God."

God not only understood Kathi's need, He understands yours! Your need may stem from an altogether different source from hers, but it is there nonetheless. You may feel anxious about life, torn between demands of time, people and money. Perhaps you feel broken and fragmented—a not-so-uncommon reaction to today's changing trends.

Fragmentation is a word used frequently by sociologists. They use it in reference to our fragmented marriages, fractured families, and ruptured relationships. What strong words to use in describing the conditions of people's lives! No wonder Jesus made the provision for us to come to Him with those things. He invites us to bring it all to Him. Whatever the problem, the invitation is to come.

He Cares, He Understands...He Hears

We know He cares, understands and hears because He invites us to cast "all your anxiety upon Him, because He cares for you" (1 Peter 5:7). The apostle was dealing with a principle that demanded action on the part of God.

The Christians of the disciples' day needed reassurance of God's caring nature. They, too, had become victims of their environment and culture. The believers were caught up in the

threat of martyrdom and reprisal from the
political leaders of their time. They were under
constant harrassment as they dealt with their
fear of the unknown. When Peter wrote to
them, he fully understood their reason for having such troubled hearts. He also knew God
was the only one who could help them.

The Lord never promises us more than He
can give! He also knows there are some things
that are much too heavy for us to carry alone.
So, when Peter invited the early Christians to
cast their cares upon God, it was because the
apostle knew God was not only concerned but
willing to help them.

The historical meaning of the word to *cast*
is an interesting one. Some religious scholars
say it is an analogy taken from the traders. The
merchants of that day used camels to carry
their heavy loads. As the animal bowed himself
low to the ground, the man carrying his burden-
some weight would bend over and with one big
heave, shift the load onto the back of the camel.

What a beautiful picture of the ability of God
to assume our burdens—and to carry them!
The question is, are we willing to hurl them onto our caring Burden Bearer?

Even though I may be fully aware of what
God can do, I can never know freedom from the
burden until it becomes His. I must accept His
invitation to cast my cares upon Him and then
believe He will stand by His promise to help.

I know, like David, that God's promises are
sure. There are three reasons we can trust Him.
First, *His promises are given out of the abun-*

dance of His resources. **Second,** *He will not quit giving until the supply runs out.* Third, *all He has to offer is potentially mine.*

When I speak of the unlimited resource of God's supply I think of Paul's words when he spoke to the church at Philippi. "God shall supply all your needs according to His riches in glory in Christ Jesus" (Philippians 4:19).

Since we know, according to Paul's words, that God gives according to *His* riches, we can be assured the supply is ample to meet the need. Note: The apostle did not say "out of" but "according to." What a difference that makes. If He were giving *out of* His abundance, the gift could be limited. As the giver, God could dole out His riches arbitrarily. But, when He promised to give *according to* His riches, the gift is based upon God's limitless supply regardless of our need.

If I were to promise to share with you according to what I have, my gift to you would be limited. However, if one of the great philanthropists of our century — Rockefeller, Kennedy, or Clements — were to make such a promise, your expectation level would rise. Both they and I may have given the same promise, and our intentions may be equally noble, but my ability to give and theirs would be measured differently.

Knowing God has promised to keep giving according to the supply, I can be sure it will never be depleted. I, then, have the written promise that He not only cares, understands, and hears, but that He also intends to *do* whatever is appropriate to provide for my needs.

James, another one of the apostles, knew exactly what Paul meant when he spoke to the early church about those anxious cares. James also knew where help came from. He tells us that "every perfect gift is from above, coming down from the Father of lights, with whom is no variation, or shifting shadow" (James 1:17).

In these days of change when people make promises they can't keep, recite vows they soon forget, and walk away from relationships without regard for each other, it is comforting to know God does not change.

I can always be sure of His promises; I can always trust in the authenticity of His Word. For He said, "Heaven and earth will pass away, but My words shall not pass away" (Matthew 24:35).

Not only do I know He cares, but I also know He understands and He hears. I can trust Him to keep His promise of being with me always. Because He touches me, I can let others know He is equally available to them.

CONTACT POINT

READ: Isaiah 43:2; 2 Corinthians 4:17; Mark 9:23; Matthew 28:18, 20

1. Who is invited to come to God? (Matthew 11:28)

2. Define the word *labor* from the context of the verse.

3. What does this say to you personally?

4. How can you help others who feel weighted down to find a release from the load of sin they might carry?

5. What responsibility do you have, according to the Great Commission in Matthew, to tell others about what Christ has done in you?

APPLIED LEARNING

Take a sheet of paper and write down the answers to the following questions.

1. List three ways in which you feel you could be more effective in your Christian testimony.

a.

b.

c.

2. How would you apply the principles we have studied here in teaching others the importance of relinquishing their burdens to the Lord?

3. Read the verses of Scripture listed below and visualize how you may appropriate them in your life.
Romans 4:21; 2 Corinthians 1:20; Psalms 34:18; 2 Peter 3:9.

4. Find someone who may not know Christ and share with him!

[1] Associated Press, ed., "Our Days Are Numbered," *Fresno Bee*, Fresno, CA, June 13, 1978.

9

To Tell Them They Are a Part of God's Plan

Inez Adair was one of the best second grade school teachers any girl could have. She made all her students feel special—including me!

I felt like I was one of her choice pupils when she came to me one day and asked me to represent the class in our school's annual speech contest. I could hardly wait to get home and tell mother about it. As soon as the classroom bell rang I ran out the door and headed toward our house.

My mom was excited for me and the days ahead were busy ones. Inez helped me with the recitation. She insisted I enunciate each word carefully and memorize the gestures to perfection. Even though Mom was sick, she, too, helped to prepare me for the big event. She sewed my dress while lying in bed, and had it ready in time for the scheduled performance.

I can still remember that beautiful rose-pink dress and how it lay in soft folds, neatly gathered around my tiny waist. I thought the day for me to wear the garment would never arrive.

Finally the day came!

A big yellow bus was waiting in the school yard to take the participants, one from each grade level, to the auditorium 25 miles away. Each of us were numbered according to age and grade. I had to wait until almost noon before my number and name were called.

When the stage monitor came after me, I reached down to pull up my long white-ribbed stockings, wanting to make very sure there were no sagging wrinkles. As I looked down I could see myself mirrored through the hard-finished shine of my shoes. I liked what I was seeing! After squaring my shoulders and drawing a quick breath, I walked onto the platform and started my monologue.

"Sue pulled her glove over her broken fingers and yelled . . ."

I grimaced, as if I were in great pain, just like my teacher had told me to do. When my eye caught Miss Adair's I could see she was pleased with what I was doing. But I was soon to discover that my teacher's approval was not enough. A friend of hers who was seated near the judge's section overheard this conversation: "The little girl in the rose pink dress is the first place winner. What shall we do? Her family is much too poor to have their child represent our county in the state finals."

I was given the lessor honor!

Losing didn't hurt nearly so much as did my feeling of rejection. The thought of not being good enough for them stayed with me for years. Now, as I think of it I am appalled at the injustice. However, I have come to realize three important things from the incident. First, my teacher chose me above all other members of the class. Second, she believed in me and was willing to take a chance on me. Third, she invested her time and energy in me.

There were times during my growing up years when I doubted my self-worth, thinking, *Since I was not good enough to represent the county in a contest, I must not be good enough for God.* During those moments I could always remind myself that there was someone who felt I was worthy of an honor — my teacher!

As a result of what Inez Adair did for me, I have since come to a better understanding of God and of how much He loves me. I didn't discover the secret overnight. It came to me in the passing years as I became aware of how God had chosen me, believed in me, and invested Himself in me!

God Chose You and Me

You may ask, "Why would God choose me?" The point is, He *did* choose you and that is an undeniable fact! When Paul wrote to the church in Ephesus, he reminded them of their position in God: ". . . according as He hath chosen us in Him before the foundation of the world" (Ephesians 1:4).

Since He does the choosing, is it not logical to believe in His choice? Because He believes in us, we can believe in ourselves — even when we disappoint ourselves.

He Chose Us and He Believes in Us

The Lord believes in us even when we fail. Remember when Peter denied Christ and said, "I do not know the man" (Matthew 26:72)? In spite of that denial at a time when the Lord needed him most, Jesus did not forget Peter. After Jesus' resurrection the angel appeared to the women at the open tomb. He said to them, "Go, tell His disciples *and Peter*, 'He is going before you into Galilee; there you will see Him" (Mark 16:7, italics added). Why would the messenger say, "and Peter"?

It must have been because the disciple was estranged from the others. He probably felt himself a loser! Yet the Lord never called him a fumbling, ineffectual failure. In fact the word failure is not to be found in the Word. It is we, not God, who confuse the act of failing with the condition of failure. Failing does not change the fact that we are chosen and that God loves us.

Timothy, the young minister who was the apostle Paul's helper, was reminded that "those who are *chosen* . . . may obtain the salvation which is in Christ Jesus and with it eternal glory . . . If we are faithless, He remains faithful; for He cannot deny Himself" (2 Timothy. 2:10, 13, italics added).

God Chose Us, Believes in Us, and Invests in Us

When God gave Jesus to die for us He gave the best heaven had, to redeem the worst of mankind. What greater investment could be made than that of giving God's own Son?

"But God demonstrates His own love toward us, in that while we were yet sinners, Christ died for us" (Romans 5:8).

He not only died for our sins, but the Lord continues to invest Himself and the quality of His nature and goodness in us. And because He does, "we have this treasure in earthen vessels, that the surpassing greatness of the power may be of God, and not from ourselves" (2 Corinthians 4:7). "In Him we have redemption through His blood, the forgiveness of our trespasses, according to the riches of His grace, which he lavished upon us. In all wisdom and insight He made known to us the mystery of His will, according to His kind intention which He purposed in Him" (Ephesians 1:7-9).

What statements of truth! They must have hit like bomb-shells on those spiritually muscle-bound Corinthians. They and the clever, indulging people from Ephesus, who felt themselves so culturally aware, needed to understand they were nothing until God invested Himself in them.

To catch the meaning of what Paul was saying, we have to consider the context in which he wrote. We know the custom of that day was to roll up valuable documents and insert them inside a bottle or vase. The purpose was to protect them from the deteriorating effects of moisture in the air.

That was also the method used in preserving the Dead Sea Scrolls. We are told when the shepherd boy unearthed the vase that was hidden beneath the rocks in a cave, he was totally unaware of the value of his findings. The value of the container holding the parchments had not yet been determined. It was not until the archaeologists discovered the contents that its worth could be declared.

Like that vase, our worth is in the treasure inside, in Christ Jesus who chooses to dwell within our earthen vessels. The container does not make the content valuable! We have no goodness of our own. We are much the same as a perfume bottle that takes its fragrance from the contents. Christians derive the *eau de cologne* of living from the aromatic bouquet of God's presence at work in us. We must let Him permeate the vessel of our lives!

Not only does He choose to reside in us, He identifies with us and is not ashamed to call us His children. "Therefore God is not ashamed to be called their God" (Hebrews 11:16).

Unfortunately, many of us go through our lives without a proper understanding of our relationship in God. We underestimate His work in us, often considering ourselves outside of His plan. Consequently, the essence of our lives is stifled by our own feelings of hopelessness and unworthiness. Barbara Holder, a young lady from North Carolina, struggled with this issue for many years. I first met her in the hospital after she had tried to commit suicide.

Barbara's small frame was silhouetted against the background of white sheets covering her hospital bed. Her eyes, red and swollen from crying, revealed the deep sorrow she felt. When I walked into the room where she lay, she shared her pain with me.

"I am deaf and the only member of my family with any hearing problem. Both of my sisters are intelligent, beautiful women. They are married, live in lovely homes and have children. Look at me! After years of working to acquire a teacher's credential, I still have nothing. My husband and I can't even have a baby. Why can't I end it all? My dreams are shattered . . . Where *is* God, anyway?"

Tears were streaming down her face—and mine! Impulsively, I pulled her tense and rigid body close to mine. She wept on my shoulder until she seemed unable to weep any more. Then, I motioned to her, asking if I might read from Psalms 139:15 (Amplified Version).

"My frame was not hidden from You, when I was being formed in secret *and* intricately *and* curiously wrought (as if embroidered with various colors) in the depths of the earth [a region of darkness and mystery]. Your eyes saw my unformed substance, and in Your book all the days *of my life* were written, before even they took shape, when as yet there was none of them."

"I see, I see," she said, pointing to herself and

back to the Bible again. *Does Barbara really understand that she, too, is a part of God's plan, that He believes in her, that she was chosen in Him, and that He wants to make an investment in her happiness?* I wondered. I left the hospital and her room without answers!

A year and a half went by before I saw or heard from her again. Then she wrote me.

> "The greatest disappointment of my life came when the doctor told me I could not bear a child. My life's desire was to raise a family — to have a home and children. When none of those things seemed to be coming to me, I lost faith in God and became jealous toward those who were blessed with those benefits.
>
> "When you came to the hospital that day, it was at a very difficult time in my life. I had just been told by another gynecologist that medical science had done all for me they could. I was at a desperate point in my life!
>
> "Thanks, Ruthe, for coming to see me. God has done a work in my heart and I have been able to understand that His plan is being developed in my life.
>
> The Lord has heard our prayers. Enclosed is a picture of our new baby, Tina. I gave birth to her just two and a half months ago. Eddy, my husband, has found a new job and we have purchased a home. We have a strong desire to reach others, to tell them God cares and that they are a part of His plan!"

Perhaps you are wondering if Barbara was healed of her deafness. No, she did not receive a physical healing. But having her spiritual ears opened, she heard! Her ears were not opened to the loud noises of the streets, but she heard the melody of a new song. Like Barbara and the blind beggar in Mark's gospel, you, too, can be twice-*touched* and *changed.* When that happens, you, too, will be ready to be *sent.*

CONTACT POINT

READ: Psalms 139; Mark 10:30; Ephesians 1:4

1. What does the Amplified Version of Psalms 139:15 say to you personally?

2. When did the Lord choose you? How does that speak to you?

3. How do you feel about your personal position in Christ (2 Peter 3:9)?

4. Do you feel yourself as a part of God's plan? If so, why and how?

5. In what way do you visualize God at work in you right now?

APPLIED LEARNING

1. Share each of the following with someone:

a. How the Lord has given you opportunities.

b. The way in which you feel He has believed in you.

c. What kind of investment He has made in you.

2. Read Psalm 139 and write down all the things that tell you what God knows about you.

3. Repeat these words daily:
I am a part of God's plan and I know He is presently at work in me!